THE SECRET
OF NEW YORK
REVEALED

THOMAS HOWARD

THE SECRET
OF NEW YORK
REVEALED

Being the Autobiographical Fragments of the Then
Recently Married
Thomas Howard Chronicling His
Numerous Discoveries
in the City of That Name

IGNATIUS PRESS   SAN FRANCISCO

Cover photograph by
Per-Eric Berglund/Getty Images

Cover design by Roxanne Mei Lum

To Lovelace,
whose strong love beckoned me from the carousel
that is New York,
towards that 'still point of the turning world'
of which Eliot speaks

and

To Gallaudet and Charles,
who, simply by being who and what they were
(and are),
filled me with sheer delight, and even happiness

CONTENTS

Foreword, by Father Benedict Groeschell   9

Prefatory Note   13

1. Summons to the Center   17
2. Sing Hey for the Law   39
3. The Styx   47
4. And Nonny for Woodstock   55
5. Vulgarity Unmasked   69
6. Of Marrows in Cream   79
7. Enter Mr. Eliot   89
8. "I Said to David Rockfeller..."   101
9. Heaven and Hell under Every Bush   109
10. The Infanta Comes   119
11. The Inexorable Summons   133
12. O Ordinariness, Where Is Thine Ordinariness   149

FOREWORD

When my friend, the fervent Catholic apologist Tom Howard, informed me that he was working on a book about his experiences while living in New York, my first reaction was: "Don't admit to anything." Tom is one of those visitors to New York who thinks that the place is something different—almost another world. I consider myself a New Yorker because I'm from Jersey City. I grew up living closer to the Statue of Liberty than almost any residents of New York City proper. Also, I think of myself as a New Yorker since I've lived here for decades, and I am defensive about our little corner of the world. We are really put off when people think that only the uneven patch of crowded streets stretching a hundred blocks from Wall Street to the urban village of Yorkville (in the East Eighties) is New York City.

Our native land is not that congested stage where outsiders come to do their thing. New York City proper is really a thousand villages, with at least another thousand surrounding it. Together they make up a metropolitan area with a population larger than half the countries in the U.N. Most of the villages and neighborhoods are very much like the rest of the United States. True, there is a wide ethnic diversity in the old neighborhoods and often an unusual combination of inhabitants. For example, there is a block in Brooklyn made up of Algonquins who work at building skyscrapers because they have no fear of heights. In Greenpoint, a most unusual neighborhood, also in Brooklyn, there's a pharmacy with a sign that tells you that they speak Polish and Slovak. Underneath this in pencil we are informed that they also speak Spanish. Apparently, no one speaks English. I myself grew up in an Irish-Jewish neighborhood where we got along famously and where life was endlessly amusing—a laugh a minute, really. The day I went to novitiate at the age of seventeen, an old Jewish lady who thought I was too young (I was) commanded her husband to take me for a walk and explain "the bees and the birds". Where else in the world but at Saint Patrick's Cathedral would Jews come into the confessional to get a blessing? Take my word for it. It's happened to me more than once.

Tom Howard, sounding a bit like those wide-eyed visitors we're familiar with, joins the throngs of people from the hinterland, which includes some of the larger cities in America, who are amazed by New York. This phenomenon has left me pondering the question: Is there really something unique about New York? It hasn't been the world's largest city for decades. The best I can do is claim that our city is the original sin capital of the world. Note well: It is not the actual sin capital, but the place where the vast majority of natives believe that there is an original sin, an inherited disaster that affects all the featherless bipeds who inhabit the uninhabitable rock of Manhattan and its environs. As one of our former mayors said, "I don't know where the world is going, but New York is there already."

If you don't believe me about original sin, come to New York on Ash Wednesday. We all get ashes—Christians, Jews, Moslems, Hindus, Buddhists, agnostics, and presumably an atheist here or there. Why? The New York answer is simple. An old Jewish lady told me, "It's free and it can't hoit." In addition, people want the priest to use the old form when imposing ashes as a reminder that we will all return to dust.

Occasionally a New Yorker will respond to this reminder with a request that their return may be as soon as possible.

Tom Howard thinks that he got a real insight into New York the night of the blackout in the '60s, when he was in the midst of millions of people without electric power, including those in elevators. I remember the night very well. I was just leaving our St. Francis Home for boys in Brooklyn when everything stopped. Being New Yorkers, we were convinced it was a snafu, an inconvenience: perhaps a mouse got into a generator—it was nothing more than that. Everyone else thought it was the beginning of a revolution or an act of terrorism. It wasn't.

New Yorkers—believers and unbelievers alike—can't stand hypocrisy. You've heard of the Bronx cheer, I'm sure. We all think that people with unabashed self-esteem are hysterically funny. Carl Rogers, the great Pelagian of the twentieth century who represented the persistent heresy that denies original sin, left New York as soon as he got his degree at Columbia and never came back. I received the same degree from the same department, but I never left town because I'm a disciple of Saint Augustine. Like all New Yorkers, I know that our hearts are restless until they rest in God.

This brings me to my final observation, one that agrees with Tom Howard. There's a lot of religion in New York, and most of it is Catholic. More than six thousand people a day enter St. Patrick's Cathedral; most of them pray, and many receive the sacraments. The city has dozens of churches open all day, and they are never empty. I suppose the passing vanity of human things is so obvious to New Yorkers that we all look for a better world and a joy that does not pass away. When the Pope comes to New York, everybody is happy except the New York Times and the Post, which, as everyone knows, are out of touch with the real people. When

Cardinal O'Connor died, the city went into mourning as it did for Cardinal Cooke before him. Even unbelieving New Yorkers hope that we Christians are right about the next life. I often think that Saint Augustine might have had a mystical insight into places like New York, or perhaps it was just his experience with ancient Rome, when he wrote that the city of God and the city of Man are "inextricably intertwined" until the end of the world. Tom Howard speaks for many when he sees this so clearly realized on the sidewalks of New York.

—Fr. Benedict J. Groeschel, C.F.R.

PREFATORY NOTE

What we have here is a period piece, so to speak. I wrote the following pages in the late nineteen-seventies, several years after my wife and I had moved to Massachusetts from New York. For some reason I fobbed the manuscript off on a former student of mine who had made himself my very own private bibliographer. He had rummaged through heaven knows how many journals, the dates of which ran back to 1965, and had assembled as exhaustive a bibliography of my "stuff" as might ever be wanted (a highly theoretical, not to say unlikely, turn of events). I had formed the habit of throwing away all the typescripts of my books (this was pre-computer) as soon as the published item appeared; but I did have a somewhat haphazard pile of my periodical writings in a box. He catalogued everything, with a solemn punctilio that still amazes me. I may add here that what files I do have are excruciatingly orderly, but that they are almost non-existent. I am compulsive, to the point of paranoia, about getting rid of paper. I would argue strenuously that all of these impressive drawers packed with paper that everyone, especially academics, amasses will only constitute a headache for whoever it is who must mop up after one dies. Certainly no one actually *consults* his files—or much of them at any rate.

In any event, having thrown away all of my book manuscripts, and having saved only the published version of the innumerable articles I had written (most of them in journals that no one has ever heard of, which all seem to have had a half-life to be measured in nano-seconds), one Christmas recently I gave my daughter the doubtful present of the whole pile of published articles. The relief of having these papers out of the house was immense. (On the same Christmas, I gave my son my whole file of "Humor", lest anyone think he was overlooked. These were items I had collected, not written.)

This left my lifetime file at a bulk of perhaps six inches. In this connection, at least, I am a happy man. But the manuscript of the book in question here: my student owned the only copy, and I had lost touch with him altogether. Twenty years passed. I fancied that he lived in New York State somewhere, but that is a large region to scour. So I rang up the alumni office of the small college where he had sat under my tutelage, and got his address. "Do you by any chance have a copy of that New York manuscript that I gave you twenty or more years ago?" "Oh yes." "Could you Xerox it for me?" "Certainly." (I paid the cost, let it be recorded.)

I am not sure what prompted me to resurrect the thing, but here it is.

I say it is a period piece. That is to dignify it. Whatever we wish to call it, I may alert the reader that the narrative—it is, actually, a rather loose narrative—is peppered with anachronisms. Anachronisms, that is, not in the sense of flaws or anomalies in the text itself, but rather in the sense of a reader's coming upon items which are long since dated. For example, New York keeps yuppifying neighborhood after neighborhood, with breathtaking speed. So places that I mention as chic, say, are now very far from being the latest thing, as it were. Restaurants suffer under the same sea-changes. Fashions, argot, political hot points, public figures—the reader must put himself in the frame of mind asked of one when one reads Trollope, say, or Henry James. (The analogy between my work and theirs obtains only in this matter of time-lapse, let it be feverishly urged before anyone forms an opinion concerning my estimate of my own work.)

There would be no point, obviously, in my offering a mere period piece to my supposititious audience. Thomas Wolfe, Marcel Proust, Vladimir Nabokov, and a hundred others have evoked the past in the course of their work, and scarcely need my help in keeping the past vivid. I suppose I would try to argue that the true substance of what is here cast in the New York of the late nineteen seventies is of a nature that has not changed qualitatively since the day after the expulsion from Eden. What was borne in upon me under the kaleidoscopic species of that city was of a piece with what T. S. Eliot called "the permanent things". The cities of the plain, with all that marks them—their fashions, their argot, their preoccupations, their amusements, controversies, and concerns—pass. But the permanent things are just that: permanent.

I think the thing that prompted me to write this account was that, against all probability (I was a scatterbrained young man in a febrile decade in an intoxicating city), I found myself, by virtue of having married the woman who is still my wife in another millennium, summoned to the Center.

Summons to the Center

The man's name was Waltz, I think. I wondered if I hadn't got it wrong, and if it wasn't really Paltz, or Platz, or Watts, or something. But it was Waltz. He was the "super", which appeared to be what New Yorkers called the building superintendents. He looked after things like the hot water, refrigerators that had gone bad, air conditioning, and noisy neighbors. I had had to ring him over some minor adjustment in a bathroom faucet and was full of apologies, sorry to bother the busy man who had twenty-one floors full, no doubt, of querulous and shrill tenants. My approach had been a timorous, "Um, I'm calling from 19G, ah, I just had a quick question about the water. No hurry at all. Just if you had a chance, sometime when you're on the floor anyway, if you could pop in and take a peek, um—I don't think it's any great problem..."

He came in wearing a madras sports jacket and a stiff, narrow-brimmed fedora made of some material compounded, it seemed, of plastic and mohair. He nursed a wet cigar stump in the corner of his mouth. I had expected someone in bib overalls. Obviously I would have to adjust my picture. It was not at all clear just what level of things one was to imagine this man as occupying and hence whether one was to think of oneself as addressing an executive or a handyman. He tinkered with the trap in the drainpipe under the washstand, but there was a faint but unmistakable suggestion of the executive in the nimbus around him, so it seemed prudent to assume that sort of hierarchy here. I was vassal, say, and he was seneschal; both of us have connections with the higher reaches of power, I the vassal/tenant by virtue of having bought rights to tenure, he the seneschal/super by virtue of his stewardship of the domain. Negotiations, difficult as they are to define, must be carried on by means of a diplomatic complex of guarded goodwill, gently applied leverage, and tacit appeal to the rights each one commands.

In any case, here he was in his madras coat on his knees under the washstand, not so much getting down to work on a job as having a look, as it were. He seemed to have a wrench somewhere about his person, though, and the problem resolved itself under his cursory executive check. He also tried the hot water tap, and in response to my exclamation of grateful awe that steaming water could be produced on the nineteenth floor of a building almost instantly, he hinted that this establishment had all sorts of clever tricks like this up its corporate sleeve. (I had supposed that one would have to wait for however long it took for the hot water to travel the whole distance through the pipes from the boiler, surely buried far below in the bowels of the building.) This was altogether the right building to have moved into: An accommodating super who would stop by in person to have a look at things, instant hot water on the nineteenth floor—Who could tell what other astonishing benefits came along with the rent here?

It was early in a hot September. My wife, whose first two names are Lovelace Claiborne (see Jamestown, Virginia), and I had arrived in town on Labor Day weekend after a splashy honeymoon all across Europe. It had been a honeymoon oddly marked by our continually running into friends—mostly my bachelor-era friends, who constituted a sampling, generally, from the bizarre end of the human spectrum. We had spent a helter-skelter weekend at a small Gramercy Park hotel in June for a day or two after the wedding, waiting for the *United States* to sail. The *France*, alas, had had an awkward set of embarkation dates, hence my having booked us into this vast floating Holiday Inn. There were, as I remember that weekend, breakfasts with this person from my days in graduate school and brunches with that person from my army days, and tea with the other person from some other epoch. An enormous group collected finally to see us to our cabin on the ship, bringing champagne; chocolates; petits fours; candied figs; and a great cone of flowers made from pink, mauve, and periwinkle-blue tissue paper. We ran into friends among the passengers as well, which raised the finely tuned question for both parties as to how convivial to be: Do they leave the honeymoon couple alone? Do we, for our part, ask them to tea or dinner on board? Two very posh old ladies in first class had us over to the dining saloon there for a laborious dinner and bingo one night.

At Le Havre an old man died in his chair on the cabin-class deck. The huge party of tourists to whom he was father, grandfather, and underwriter was plunged into dolor and shock and spent the day hurriedly canceling their entire European tour and arranging their sad return to America.

Lovelace and I picked up a small Hillman station wagon in Southampton and recrossed the Channel to France on a boat full of draggled and vaguely sick English trippers, most of whom seemed to be young mothers in limp, sleeveless jersey blouses pushing infants in strollers. These latter on the whole had strawberry ice cream dribbling down their chins.

We raced through Paris; picnicked on bread, cheese, and wine among the poppies beside the road in the Loire Valley; crossed the Saint Bernard Pass with its cantilevered concrete canopies put up over the road to keep the avalanches from burying the motorists; and spent a sybaritic week at a hotel in Elba where they answered the phone with "Pronto, pronto!" when you rang through to room service, and they brought your morning tea up to your little terraced villa in a pot that had long been used for brewing coffee. Then on through Tuscany, with its silvery gray-green trees, to Florence, with its Ghiberti doors, its Medici tombs, its David, its churches and palaces, and its wonderful warm tan stuccoed walls with their apricot-colored shutters and awnings. Rome, where the Apostolic See reigns amid mighty Renaissance splendors atop the ruins of the caesars. Greece, with soft purple olives, meats wrapped in grape leaves, retsina wine, broken marble, caryatids, the Oracle, Olympus; Yugoslavia, with beautiful bronzed children waving energetically from the roadside and all your Western European languages useless in ordering lunch; Bulgaria—ten minutes across the border just to say we have been in Bulgaria; Hungary and Budapest, with its lovely wide tree-lined boulevards empty of private cars, its museum full of Rembrandt drawings, and balalaikas plinking and strumming in the restaurants. Then Austria: back in the light of day on this side of the Iron Curtain, one felt; Austria, with its Mozart, its churches in all their baroque scramble of painted plaster, reliquaries, baldachinos, stoups, monstrances, and altars, and its black fir trees, steep green fields, and peaks; then the Rhine Valley, then Belgium, then— ah, then—England. Home. They speak English here. A small inn near Ipswich, suggested hesitantly by a woman at a filling station as perhaps "a bit pricey", where the waiter suggests a fried breakfast: sausage, bacon, eggs, mushrooms, grilled tomatoes, fried bread, toast in a rack, Marmite, marmalade, and a pot of tea, all on a white cloth, with a neatly trimmed flower garden outside the window. Home, home, home.

On to Norwich that morning, where I am to be best man at the wedding of a friend who is marrying the Archdeacon's daughter. Hence it will be in the cathedral, and the Lord Bishop himself will marry them. We drove along the little roads of East Anglia that morning toward Norwich. We had been married perhaps six weeks now. Here I come, a married man, with my lady by my side, to assist at the nuptial mysteries of my friend. This lady who has been beside me in this car for these peripatetic weeks through all that strange and remote terrain—who is she? Who is she, so pretty and fresh every morning in her summery flowered frocks and matching shoes? Who is this, who has come with me on this odyssey? Why should she entrust herself to my planning and my driving on those right-hand-drive European roads in this strange car built for left-hand-drive English roads? Who is she who has packed her suitcases so economically, so that her groom will not have mountains of luggage to wrestle with, but who nonetheless appears every night as we retire in a new gown and peignoir, all fragrant, feminine, angelic? What could she say to this other lady who is herself now to approach her husband at the high altar? Nay, some things cannot quite be told, either because there is no warrant to dole them out or because they won't yield themselves to any conceivable telling. What is it, this coming together of the man and the woman? My lady, a good and wise woman, knew in the marrow of her bones, long before I did, what it was all about. (It would take years for the splendor of the mystery to percolate through the almost impermeable fabric of my being.)

We knew that my friend, an architect, was to be working at the abbey church at Wymondham that morning. We came along the lane between the hedgerows next to the abbey and were hailed by a great shout from the sky. There he was, standing on top of the abbey tower, waving. That's as it should be, I thought—where else would he be, and how else would I want my wife to have her first glimpse of him. His own drawings and designs had always been full of angels and archangels and all the company of heaven, blowing about in an ecstatic divine tempest above silos and farm buildings where the ordinary work of life went on: the commonplace shot through with glory. The humdrum as a mode of bliss. The antiphon between farmyards and heaven. And here he is, shouting down to our station wagon in the lane from the top of the abbey. Hey, nonny. Gloria.

We wore dove-gray morning dress with gray top hats and gloves for the wedding (the only time in my life I will ever appear in this noble array, I thought). The bridal procession came down the long nave aisle, with the Bishop in his great brocaded cope, the ecclesiastical attendants, the bridal attendants, and the bride on the arm of her father, who, by virtue of his office as archdeacon, wore gaiters—a kind of sacerdotal puttees wholly unfamiliar to Americans.

What was going on there, I have often wondered in my reveries since then. What was that gorgeous charade? What shall I say to my children when I show them the photographs in my album from that day: the view of the procession taken from the dizzy height of the clerestory of the Cathedral Church of the Holy and Undivided Trinity in Norwich, or the high altar with the Saxon throne above it, or the Norman arches of the ambulatory, or the merry crowd with champagne glasses aloft in the garden of the archdeaconry afterward, with the best man (that's me there up on the chair) toasting the very good health of his lordship the Bishop on his birthday, which happened to be on that same

day? How shall I tell my children—schooled as they are by
their generation that the great thing is to strive for natural-
ness and spontaneity—how shall I tell them what this was all
about? What on earth are these ranks of Norman and Gothic
arches? What is this long nave? What this thunderous organ
music and these brocades, and this altar and throne? And
why this lady all gowned and veiled in white? Why is she led
along this way on the arm of her father and then handed
over to the arm of her groom? And why are we all standing
by, attending on the business?

Will I be able to get it through to my small son and daughter that all this egregious ritual and structure may be, lo and
behold, lo and behold, far, far closer in to the center of things
than any hunkered-down, blue-jeaned, guitar-serenaded,
beach wedding with the vows cobbled up by the pair in question? Here in this cathedral it is no cute little trial relationship we are agreeing to begin for as long as we both shall
love. It is no housekeeping plan being inaugurated with a
fifty-fifty scheme in mind for dividing up lawnmowing, dish-
washing, and careers. It is no open marriage, with brisk agree-
ments that each partner shall be free to establish this liaison
and that one if it looks fun and healthy, all of us all the while
being very grown up and very sensible about these things.
No. No, no, no. If the charade—this ancient charade, marked
similarly in a hundred centuries in a thousand cultures—if it
means anything at all, it means that this man and this woman
are stepping up into a great mystery, much greater and more
splendid than either of them has any notion of at this point;
and that they enter together, with heads bowed in obedience to the rubric, to find out just what it is all about and
how it happens that freedom and wholeness for both of them
lie, oddly enough, along a way already well trodden and well
marked with the rules of the road. This woman, all decked

in demure white: Is she not for the moment *all* women? This ceremonial array: Does it not bespeak something that is close to the center of things, but that we cannot, in the hurly-burly of ordinary daily life, with its shopping bags and laundry and diapers, always quite catch? We need this highly conscious, highly structured, *ritual* enactment of what is always there—that a woman is a noble creature, bearing as she does the image of God, and that at her approach to her lord, the other one who bears the image of God, it is well that the mystery of her being and of her approach be veiled and clothed in white. We need this to bring home to us what is at stake here. Ceremonies matter. Ancient ceremonies matter. (They weren't dreamed up yesterday over a Coke or pasted together in a sharing session.) They come from the sources of human imagination responding to the biggest mysteries there are.

And all these friends here: What are we doing, all standing about? Are we not signaling to the bride and groom, and to all who wish to know, and to the hosts of heaven, that this is no private transaction? It is preeminently public, that is, human. Here we announce our solidarity one with another, all of us. We wait upon this man and this woman as they step into this most private, most public, act. We stand about them, bringing in our bodies the whole human race to the spectacle. The ceremony needs us, too.

Hence these bridesmaids, who have no doubt shared many a tousled, barefooted lark with the bride. Now they come, themselves decked in fine raiment, stepping punctiliously down the long aisle, not capering, not calling to one another or to the bride, not waving greeting to friends in the congregation. Why all this solemnity? Why are they suddenly cut off from us, who know them perfectly well? Why can't we pinch them or clap them on the back now?

Because. Because. There is something else going on now. This ritual carries us through the clutter and random tumble to the awareness that in the "ordinary" business of boys and girls, or of men and women, we are close to the central mystery of the Creation (male and female created he them), and that this is a mystery worth pausing over and marking on such an occasion. Pinches and claps on the back are fine, but you pause when you look into the shrine. You stop frolicking momentarily. These young women now bear a heavy and glorious ceremonial weight upon them. They are not particularly Jane and Meg and Kate now: they are Jane and Meg and Kate appearing as attendant womanhood, assisting at the holy mysteries.

And the Bishop. Here is the Church Catholic—the paradigm of humanity: men and women who live in the clutter of ordinariness, but who perceive in that clutter the harbingers of glory and who offer it all up daily in sacrifice to the Throne. This merely biological event down here, then—this man and this woman deciding to cohabit: the Church sees the biology as an epiphany of what is true and marks, announces, and hallows it publicly. The Bishop in his cope: he is not just Launcelot (although that was, happily, his name). He, like everyone else here, bears a particular burden in this ceremony, gloriously wrought in his episcopal vestments, ring, and crozier. We need to see this, we Christian men and women with eyeballs through which we look out and see the world ordered in colors and shapes and textures. The *idea* is all very well and good; but the idea needs to be embodied for us, presented to us, as, once, the Word presented itself to us in flesh.

Then the recessional. I stood aside and watched as my friend turned to his lady and, with a courteous and medieval gesture, placed her hand on the back of his own hand, raised

it high, and himself standing aside as it were, led her, crowned
with joy, down the steps from the chancel, through the choir,
where we were all gathered, under the great organ screen,
and down the long nave aisle to the west door. The strag-
gling tourists who had happened into the nave during the
solemnities stood hesitant and fumbling at this sudden celestial pageant coming across their Tuesday morning tour
schedule.

From Norwich we drove to London, then to North Wales
(tea with friends at their tiny stone cottage, with thin strips
of buttered bread, savouries, jam tarts, berries, and cream),
on through the Lake District on a drizzly Sunday morning,
to the West Highlands of Scotland. A tiny inn at Applecross
at the end of a ribbon of road that climbed over the rocky
glens, looking across the water to Raasay and Skye; a bed-
and-breakfast cottage near the bridge of Orchy, where something brought hysterical laughter on us as we lay under the
feather bed, and we laughed so hard and so long that the
goodwoman asked us the next morning if everything was all
right. Edinburgh, peering at the spot on the floor in Holy-
rood Palace where they stabbed David Rizzio to death; and
Marlene Dietrich one evening at the Festival, trailing mysterious and witching clouds of femininity and all the inter-
continental enchantments of *The Blue Angel* and Hemingway
that her life has entailed.

Thence to New York and the hunt for an apartment in
the simmering heat of Labor Day weekend, when the whole
city has gone to Asbury Park, Fire Island, or at least Jones
Beach. The scramble for places to live in the city is a finely
tuned scramble. You have to get three elements into equi-
poise: you need to find (1) *what* you want (2) *where* you want
it, (3) at a *price* you can contemplate. Do you want a "floor-
through" in a brownstone, a mews loft, a cellar, or a pent-

house? Do you want to be in Chelsea, Upper Broadway, Murray Hill, the West Village, or Park Avenue? Can you manage $250 a month? (That was the mid-sixties: such a figure would arouse only incredulous stares now.) The great trick is to locate what you want in the Sunday *Times* real estate section and get over there before all the other young types who are also hunting for places to live arrive. So it is a question of getting a copy of the *Times* as soon as it appears on Saturday night and boring through column after column of minuscule boxes describing one Shangri-La after another, circling the few that look likely, then waiting for the earliest possible hour on Sunday morning, when owners might be expected to be awake and recovered from hangovers and ready to receive inquiries. Then it's taxis and subways and running, paper in hand, into neighborhoods you will never see again, up steps, and into the place with other early inquirers, who eye you balefully, then out again.

We finally triumphed by finding on Fourteenth Street, just off Fifth Avenue, a nice, clean modern apartment in a building called The Parker Gramercy. The Parker Gramercy, I thought: that sounds posh. We must have found something good here. There was a huge, breathless sign on top of the building proclaiming in letters you could see from the Hudson River, "NOW RENTING!" Heavens! I thought. We'd better hurry. Clearly it has just been opened up to the public, and only the agile few will get in. There was a florid man in a sports shirt sitting at a little table in the lobby reading a newspaper when I rushed in. No other inquirers were about. He turned out to be more than accommodating and seemed glad to help us negotiate this precarious and fortunate rental.

We moved in. We had an ironing board and a mattress for furniture, as I remember the first days. Then a station wagon load of oddments arrived, and we bought dishcloths, eggbeaters, scouring pads, and wooden spoons at John's Bargain Store directly across 14th Street. In the early weeks of settling in, we began to notice a curious number of new buildings just like ours, with posh-sounding titles, all of them declaring themselves to be Now Renting, and all of them, clearly, half empty. All of them seemed to have been built on streets that were singularly lacking in the little elements of charm that experienced New Yorkers become astute at recognizing: such tokens as sycamore trees planted along the sidewalks, brownstone fronts redone, geranium boxes under the windowsills, glossy black wrought-iron railings—that sort of thing. Our building and the hundreds like it all over the city opened out onto streets lined with John's Bargain Stores, cut-rate furniture emporia, and the A&P.

It takes a heap more than livin' to make an apartment a home in New York. If it is in an old building or a brownstone, you have decades of grease, grit, and paint to scour and chip away at. If it is new, you have death-white paperthin walls, pinkish electroplated bogus-copper doorknobs, and aluminum window frames to do something about. We bought huge oak shutters at Bloomingdale's, painted them coral and antiqued them with umber, and got Mr. Waltz and his maintenance men to drill holes in the concrete outer walls for the screws and hinges to hang these timbers on. There is a type of plastic plug that you buy at a hardware store and sink into the drill holes in a concrete wall, the idea being that this will receive a wood screw. My difficulty with these plugs was twofold: either the plug went awry as I was pounding it into the hole, and I ended up with a hole jammed with mutilated plastic; or the screw turned out to be too long, and I found myself wrenching the screwdriver around, chewing up the slot in the head of the screw. Besides attaching the shutters to the walls, I had to join the panels in these shutters to each other, and I counted 132 holes and brass screws for these hinges. There was always something vaguely homemade looking about the whole assemblage after I got it up, but within a few weeks Lovelace had touched the apartment with a warm, Gallo-Florentine touch, and the people who came to dinner did not have to eat off the card table.

We bought a Yorkshire terrier named Thrumply Quodles. He looked like a dog you might see in a painting of Eleanor of Aquitaine. He would find a patch of morning sunlight on the rug and settle into it with minuscule princeliness. It struck me that he was doing the will of God. Here was a creature whose appointment was to bear about in his being this kind of perfection and no other. He had only one task to do, and he did it well. He bore his part in the Creation obediently and simply. No other creature in all of heaven or earth could bear the particular form of excellence appointed to the Yorkies to bear.

Often in the evenings we would walk down into Greenwich Village. Fourteenth Street, where we lived, forms a sort of northern extremity to the Village, like some Great Wall running through the hinterland steppes on the edge of the empire. You always felt as though you were walking into more civilized terrain as you got down toward West Tenth Street and on down to Sheridan Square. At least we did in those early days. Later, after we had moved uptown, those Village reaches seemed grubby and spurious.

There was a small Italian restaurant on MacDougall Street where you could get piping hot canelloni, manicotti, or fettucini (all new to me: I never could keep straight which was which and still can't), a green salad, and a glass of wine for about two dollars. Sometimes before we ate we would go to a late afternoon showing of a Bogart or Garbo film in one of the numberless little cinemas in the Village. There were no babysitters to worry about yet, and our schedule was our own. My graduate classes at New York University in Washington Square met only once weekly each, at off hours like 4:00 or 6:00 P.M.

It was a simple sort of existence generally. New Yorkers become adept at defining for themselves a simplicity like this. It is necessary as a defense against the maelstrom of sheer multiplicity that is New York. Here you are with everything dinning at you, spinning about your ears, shimmering and coruscating in front of your eyes, bidding for your participation. Every imaginable kind of enterprise, vocation, pastime, indulgence, diversion, exploration, discovery. Ten thousand worlds justling and clamoring: teamsters and their Mack trucks shouting and banging at loading platforms in the West Twenties; beige-carpeted galleries on upper Madison Avenue offering paintings and sculptures to tax the taste of the most urbane jade; Orthodox Jews with long black coats, white socks, and curls at their temples going to *shul*; frankfurter vendors with blue-and-yellow umbrellas over their little steaming carts at a hundred street corners; burly, tanned, horn-rimmed, putty-eyed men and their besequined, becoiffed women, just back from Miami Beach, tipping doormen at East Side restaurants and imperiously expecting cabs; the despondent thousands in the Lexington Avenue subway, or the lone souls in the dun murk of the Eighth Avenue line; bony, blonde, tanned Saxon matrons with faces that have been to a thousand parties in Bar Harbor, Oyster Bay, and Hobe Sound; students, tycoons, derelicts, musicians, secretaries, tourists, freaks, priests, dropouts, kids; all of them bibbed and tucked and Afro'd and begoggled and unbra'd and hiked up and decked and vested and jeaned. Hey, hey, hey.

And there are all the things to do. Brunch at the Rainbow Room or the Côte Basque. Courses in psycholinguistic self-transcendence or Serbo-Croatian soup cookery at odd little night classes. Peep shows, massages, and porno shops on Forty-Second Street. Cantatas, motets, and organ recitals in a score of churches on Sunday afternoon. Salmon, flowers, cheese, and baguettes to buy at tiny shops; and vegetables at open stands banked with eggplants, artichokes, endives, avocadoes, pomegranates, and melons. The Frick, the Plaza, the Whitney, the Met, City Center, Broadway, off-Broadway, off-off Broadway, the Thalia (old Eisenstein films), Central Park, Wall Street. Hey, hey, hey.

We were young, new, and childless. Here is this great Babylonian oyster to be pried open by us. (This line of thought ran, I think, more through my mind than through Lovelace's. I would scan the columns of outré offerings in *The Village Voice* and think to myself, "Mm. We must try that one of these days.") But you can't live with Everything. So New Yorkers find various ways of achieving a chic and self-conscious simplicity. They walk to work instead of coping with the vagaries of the subway. They eschew the West Side. They eschew the East Side. They never go to restaurants. They go only to little untouristy restaurants. They hire private cars to avoid the taxi struggle. They steal away to Sag Harbor or Litchfield for weekends. They see "only a few close friends".

After pursuing films, small restaurants, big concerts at Carnegie Hall and Philharmonic Hall, and small concerts at churches like Saint George's Stuyvesant Square (whose reach exceeded its grasp, musically), plus the ballet, plays, and musicals, for a year or so, we whittled it down to the two operas. Seldom after our first two years in the city did we go out at night except to dinner with friends or to the opera. The New York City opera productions were vigorous, agile, and muscular. They seemed to be the Avis to the Met's Hertz.

We liked their productions much better than the Met's, but of course you got to hear Birgitt Nilsson, Leontyne Price, Joan Sutherland, and Franco Corelli at the Met, and you can't fault that. When we first started going, Beverly Sills was singing the Queen of the Night (only two arias the whole evening) in the New York City Opera production of *The Magic Flute*. Nobody knew who she was. As her career shot up and everyone took notice of her, we could murmur contentedly, "Yes, of course. She's our girl. We used to hear her when the rest of you had never heard of her. We've watched her all the way along."

Both operas, as well as Balanchine's New York City Ballet and the Philharmonic, were housed at Lincoln Center at Ninth Avenue and Broadway. Half the business of going to the opera was the arriving and the intermission, which is as it should be, no doubt. All the best things in life are set about and decked appropriately: people's birthdays, peace treaties, Nobel Prizes, the Eucharist. We don't want naked prizes—bare diamonds, or diplomas sent through the mail. We need to have these worthy things decked.

Opera, we found, is elaborately decked. The sweep of the terrace and fountain, all flooded with light at night, with the Metropolitan Opera House looming in thunderous travertine enormity across the end, warmed with the pink Chagall murals inside, visible through the glass-arched facade; limousines and taxis driving up, and crowds emerging from the subway entrances; everyone up the steps outside and across the red-carpeted foyer to stalls, boxes, mezzanine, or upper circles. Everything is red and gold inside the auditorium itself: red plush seats and a general look of gold everywhere else.

Just before it is time for the overture to begin, the six or eight crystal chandeliers that hang from the immense height of the ceiling begin to rise ever so slowly, at the same time dimming gradually. You move across a dramatic psychological and mythopoeic frontier now. You go from the hither side, which is all festivity, chatter, lights, purses, bustle, arrivals, and expectation, to the far side, where the opera lies. The overture is the border. When it begins, we here in the audience become spectators. Up to now we have looked at each other. Here we are, the hardy troops of opera regulars, all serious business; the splashy groups in the boxes and on the aisles for whom it is primarily an outing; the music students with their scores, peering down from the gallery, happily aware that they alone, of the whole throng here tonight, are the ones who really know what is going on—what Donizetti is going to do next, and how Sutherland's mad scene compares with Galli Curci's, and what John Nelson is going to demand of the orchestra; and the lithe and languid young men, all got up in Cardin and Bill Blass, who seem to have come with the idea in mind mainly of draping themselves at the bar at intermission time with champagne and 120-centimeter cigarettes.

Up to now we have all been busy looking at each other or at the program notes and plot summary. (Opera plots are so complicated, and so like each other, that it is nearly impossible to remember who broke whose heart, and who took revenge on whom, in a given opera.) Now, in darkness, we in the audience cease to exist. A line has been drawn, and we cross it. With the darkening of the lights and the beginning of the overture, our whole corporal existence here in these seats is swallowed up in the spectacle. Eyes and ears are all. The darkness is necessary for the spell to work. The music is necessary. The footlights are necessary; the curtain is necessary. Indeed, it is necessary that this curtain be huge and gold and that it be gathered up just so, with the rich folds crinkling heavily as it rises. And the sets revealed as the curtain goes up are necessary.

The stage may be virtually bare, or it may be crowded with laughing, bosomy French girls in flouncy skirts carrying great wide, shallow baskets of flowers and fruit: that part does not matter. Or rather it does matter, since it is this very bareness or plenitude on stage that tells us where we are. The overture has anticipated the whole drama, with its lyric, dancing flutes, or its ominously shuddering strings, or its horns blatting out doom. Now the sets carry us one step further into the drama. We know that gaiety, intrigue, love, and death will unfold for us.

But what on earth are we doing here? Who can believe all this shameless nineteenth-century trumpery? No dragoons have ever rushed about through darkened Parisian streets with swords waving like that. No maidens have ever perished with such coloratura passion. No fathers have ever remonstrated with such baritone bravura. What are we telling ourselves here? We have paid forty dollars for these two seats, and have undertaken the daunting cross-Manhattan journey, and have set aside an entire evening—for this. What can it all mean?

Well, I thought, it has something to do with what we mortal men are. We all pass through experiences (hunger, desire, fear, passion, death), but, unlike dogs, who also pass through these experiences, we men need to have them all re-presented to us. We need to be hailed, as it were, with the *spectacle* of passion, or jealousy, or victory, at one remove, so that we can *see* it. When we are embroiled directly in the experience, the way Lucia and Tamino are, up there on the stage, we don't have any leisure to reflect on it. We can't see any shape to it all. We can't get any purchase on it. We have no perspective. But lo, by means of this absurd music here, and this extravagant spectacle, we find the whole business lifted away from the ad hoc clutter of mere happening, and placed where we can now see it. The experiences themselves that the characters up on stage there are shouting so gloriously about are completely familiar to us all. We are not discovering any new data by coming here. We are having the familiar stuff given back to us, and we find the experience of this to be ravishing.

Mm. Yes. That is the job that all art does, isn't it? What else? Why go to a museum and look at a picture of a man and a maid in a rowboat when you can see the same thing in three dimensions outside the museum in Central Park, or better still, when you can hire a rowboat yourself and take her for a ride? Or why go all the way to Florence to look at an enormous naked marble boy when you can see a hundred real ones in any locker room?

Well, we need to have it *shown* to us. The immediate and "real" experience of being in a rowboat with a girl is, oddly, opened up and somehow glorified for us by virtue of Renoir's painting. And our vision of the human form is intensified and vivified when it is taken, isolated, and held in absolute repose there in Michelangelo's *David*. We can't quite get it when we are in the boat or the locker room ourselves.

And here in this opera house, with all of the goings-on there on the stage—this breathless apprehension, these supplications, these beggings of help from heaven, these shattered loves, these desolations: Do not these tumultuous tenor and soprano arias blast open our ordinarily cramped capacity to experience these emotions? Isn't all this noise and spectacle and action a way of decking these terrific human experiences in a manner appropriate to the enormity of those experiences? In "real" experience, it all comes at you in a clutter, and there's no time to collect your wits, and your emotions rage and fling and grasp at straws, and all is what

T. S. Eliot called "a general mess and imprecision of feeling". But here, sitting in these red plush seats without actually facing a furious rival or getting a secret note announcing our lady's perfidy, we can for a moment get some perspective on human experiences. We are far enough away from the business to do so. We have a leisure we don't have when we are in the middle of it.

It is as though the sheer *size* of human emotions is presented to us in these exaggerated situations. (Not many of us have had to duel for our love. Not many of us have had to pick our way through the intrigues of a masked ball in the course of our courtship. But we have all known the perils of love and the finely tuned necessities of love. That is what is dramatized up there in those outrageous situations. Our emotions and experiences are there in full costume.) In real life we are bundled headlong through things, and who has the chance to catch his breath, let alone respond, to things?

But here, in this deafening aria, bellowed from the cavernous lungs of Franco Corelli—those lungs that have been bullied for years so that they are strong enough to do this vicarious service for us here in the audience—here we find what we needed in our own agony. This says it exactly. *That's* how I felt and didn't have time to know it; it was all so horrible and cluttered. Ah! Yes! Yes—that's it! Oh, yes— right on up there onto that B-flat—YES! Oh, sing it, you angel! Sing it! Now we're getting to the heart of the matter. This is what it's all about. Here's why we paid our $40 and put on our best clothes and toiled across Manhattan. Here's why we're all here in this ostentatious emporium. It's because human experience is this big and this splendid. Oh, we're not dogs, left blinking vacantly at slammed doors, or hogs snuffling under hedges. Oh, no: we are men and women. Gods, we have been called, and heaven knows we feel things the way the gods do, and there's never enough room for the feelings.

But wait. Surely that can't be it? Surely we can't argue that we all come here just to get our chaotic emotions sorted out. This has got to be more than just a lavish rite for the exorcism of the demons in our breasts?

It is more, of course. It is not that I need actually to have been stung into a jealous rage two weeks ago in order for me to appreciate this opera. On that accounting we would all be left out of a great many operas, and of most dramas into the bargain. Isn't it too paltry to see opera as a place where we can purchase a sort of luxurious purgation for our feelings?

Yes and no. The most ancient authority on questions like this (Aristotle) argued that this purgation *is* part of the value of the thing. But there is more. It is that here we are hailed with beautifully wrought representations, not just of our own private experiences but also of *human* experience. Just as liveried heralds blared "The King!" with silver flourishes, so this fanfare here blared "Man!" to me. It is no beggar or poltroon on stage up there. It is a splendid creature, bearing the imago Dei and capable of enormous emotions. And since that creature is no longer decked in the godlike nakedness that adorned him in Eden, we do well to array him in all the panoply we can amass. Ermine, scarlet, and gold for the King. Scenery, violins, and sopranos for us all.

Something like this, one thought, was going on at the opera.

2

Sing Hey for the Law

It happened to be the year for the mayoralty campaign when we moved to New York. The Democratic candidate was a person called Beame who some years later did, in fact, become mayor. But not that year. The populace appeared to feel that the wheels of the Democratic chariot were driving heavily and that what New York needed was a brisk new start. The Republicans promised such a new start in the person of Mr. John Lindsay.

It is more than odd that a Republican should even appear on the ballot in New York, since that city has long since abandoned every single political notion that the Republican party ever pretended to espouse. But politics in New York are themselves more than odd, and you find that a man (Lindsay, for example) may advance his name under the Republican ensign all the while holding a political viewpoint some miles to the left of Trotsky. (New Yorkers are a wry species politically, and if Ivan the Terrible chose to run for the Peasants' Egalitarian Caucus, no one would descry an anomaly.)

Lindsay seemed to be the thing we all wanted. He was young, blue eyed, lean, and tousle-haired (we were still aflush with the Kennedy afterglow then), and he managed to disarm everyone with his candor. He would appear in the streets of Harlem with his shirtsleeves rolled up above his elbows, the idea being, "We've got tough work to do, right, gang? Never mind about coats and ties and limousines and walnut desks in City Hall, then."

New Yorkers believe this sort of thing, and the *New York Times* more than them all. Pictures were rushed onto the front pages. The word was passed in the chic, rumpled circles of liberal journalism, academia, and proletaria: Lindsay's the man!

It was all very heady. Doctrinaire Democrats who had never met a Republican found themselves atingle with the idea of pulling the lever for one of these creatures. What fun! Here, from that sluggish antediluvian jumble of political troglodytes springs Saint George himself! Fancy voting for a Republican!

Everyone was terribly earnest. Jews, Irish, Italians, Latins, blacks, and the Anglo-Saxons who tried to be hearty and liberal from their townhouses in the East Sixties: all the troops, trusty and undoubted, that the Democratic party can ordinarily count on. Everyone was on the march. It was a crusade. We've got to stand tall, all of us serious, selfless, concerned, *good* people, and advance. We must pluck down the basilica of power, privilege, and influence; drag the sweating and oleaginous politicians from their swivel chairs; fling open the doors; and let the people in.

The picture is a winning one. It gets to looking more like a May dance than a military advance, what with hippies and their homespun girls, tousled professors from Columbia, Episcopal seminarians, reporters, fashion models, charwomen, Quakers and Unitarians, and all the others who show up for enlightened causes all linking arms and capering forth; everyone's breast is swelling with virtue.

The challenger to all this was William F. Buckley. Buckley with his dry, urbane wit. Buckley with his pencil, clipboard, and well-placed "uhs" skewering floundering liberals on his

TV program. Buckley seen at stoplights around town on his motor scooter. Buckley whose very name brought a glaze of baleful and incredulous contempt into the eyes of all enlightened New York liberals.

The difficulty about Buckley was that everyone had the uneasy hunch that he was getting closer to the truth of the matter than anyone else. Free from the burden of a possible victory in November and hence of having to cultivate irreconcilable voting blocs, he chipped and hacked away at the barnacles on the hull politic, where other candidates had to dab away with flannel and warm suds, sedulously trying to make their efforts appear plausible. Poverty, filth, inflation, the labor hegemony, crime, transit, taxes, welfare: all the topics that bedevil New York civilization. Buckley insisted morning, noon, and night that the way out of it all might just possibly lie in a retreat from some of the avenues that had landed the whole enterprise in the current bog and in an effort to discover a firmer, and entirely different, footing.

But this sort of radicalism is called reaction by New Yorkers and gets a candidate nowhere. No one supposed for a moment that Buckley would win, least of all Buckley himself. (Upon being asked what he would do first if he won, he remarked, "Demand a recount.") The great fear was that he would siphon enough Republican votes away from Lindsay to hand the whole thing to Beame.

Everyone's fears were groundless. Lindsay won (handily, as I remember). I was jubilant. The year 1965 was for me about the fifth in a rather spotty effort on my part to make myself a liberal while still prudently holding onto principles that, I suspected, reached to the roots of Creation. It cannot be done, but I did not know that then. Here was our man, and he has galvanized all these wonderful people into a coalition for righteousness. Hosanna! If not quite *Benedictus qui*

venit in nomine Domini, at least blessed is he that cometh in
the name of the people. If not garments and palm branches,
at least confetti and champagne.

New York, however, turns out to be intractable eventually to all measures designed for her rescue. Alaric the Visi-
goth, Suleiman the Magnificent, Ghengis Khan, Frederic
Barbarossa, nay, Attila the Hun himself—their names would
be lost to history if they had had to begin in New York.
Draconian measures do no good. The superscription over
the door of hell seems hardly more bleak than the "abandon
hope" written over this political door.

The crusade disappeared into the fen.

Oh, to be sure, here was Mr. Lindsay, and there was Mr.
Lindsay, now with a manifesto, again with a pact, yet again
with a promise. But things kept vanishing somewhere between the municipal corridors, the union headquarters, and
the Mafia. New Yorkers, like puppies watching their play-
mates disappear down the street to school, wagged their tails
more and more feebly. The columnists, all adulation and zeal
during the campaign, grew testy. Nobody said anything about
Mr. Lindsay yet. Give him time. If Joan of Arc goes out to
battle, at least give the girl time. If you send the children off
to the Crusade, don't expect tidings tomorrow.

But the traffic kept jamming, and the soot kept falling,
and the rents kept rising, and the unions kept demanding,
and the Lexington Avenue subway kept halting unaccount-
ably between stops until one fine morning it halted altogether. The transit workers—all of them—had gone on strike.
Not only had they gone on strike; they had struck in defi-
ance of a court order. "The judge can drrrop dead in his
black rrrobes", snapped the union chief.

Spots swam before my eyes. My viscera trembled loose
from their moorings. What is happening? I wondered. This

is unprecedented, surely. Am I the only civilized man left in town? Call out the militia! Get the cossacks! Shoot your way through the lines and man the buses and subways with legionnaires! We can't live with this! This is—it's *anarchy*!

What I did not know then was that New Yorkers will, in fact, live with anything. Their docility makes shorn sheep look positively bristling. There is no levy that New Yorkers will not absorb. There is no burden that they will not let you pile on their already toppling load. Like North African burros, they totter along, their heartbreaking asininity glimmering from their meek eyes.

I found this out during the subway strike. Everyone—the mayor, the *New York Times*, and the people you met at cocktail parties—huffed and puffed, decried everything, deplored everything, pontificated, solemnly pronounced the situation intolerable—and meekly walked to work. The mayor, as I remember it, was photographed walking from Gracie Mansion to City Hall, a walk of perhaps three miles. Luckily my own walk was about six blocks long. I had begun my graduate studies, and New York University in Washington Square was just down Fifth Avenue from our apartment. During the strike I used to see if I could walk the entire way without seeing the traffic on Fifth Avenue move an inch. I usually won my wager. You could stand on a corner and look in any one of the four directions and see four rivers of immobile cars, stretching like glaciers as far as you could see. There sat the drivers, stultified, docile, gazing through their windshields. It was not at all clear to me what they thought they were doing: Clearly there was no question of traffic's *going* anywhere, so what had they told themselves as they got into their cars that morning? One would have thought that driving was a form of transport wholly unsuited to the situation, like trying to hike up Everest in dancing pumps. A bad choice.

Things happen to your outlook during times like this. You learn, for a start, that history does muddle on. Apocalypse is not, after all, under every bush. You and everyone else absorb outrage after outrage, and the only thing that happens is that you all get slightly wearier and more blasé. Your threshold of shockability goes up. It takes more to rouse you now. You also learn that public rhetoric is like a wind tunnel: it blows and blows, ever so ferociously, but nothing happens to the surrounding terrain.

While the rhetoric raged, and the panel of mediators worked in their shirtsleeves day after day and night after night, I wondered what was happening to the people whose livelihood depended on the working of the transit system, but who were not being paid any union strike wages. What about the people who ran the little flower kiosks down in the subway stations? And the newsstand vendors down there? To say nothing of the thousands who lived in Jamaica, Queens, and Brooklyn, who could not possibly get to Manhattan to open up their shops and stands all over town and who thereby lost days' worth of the only income they had. These were the people who were being ground to mincemeat, it seemed to me. The rich ride out any storm there is, and the middle classes manage fairly well somehow. (*We* certainly weren't hurting: for one thing, we didn't need a ride anywhere.) But it seemed to me that somebody owed some hundreds of millions of dollars to these people who were being made to pay dearly for public disorder.

That was the rub, of course. Disorder. And no chance of anyone's calling order out of it, least of all the mayor. I had blithely assumed that there is always law to fall back on and that short of full-dress insurrection with bombing and shooting there is no such thing as public collapse. But clearly I had been whistling in the dark. You can have all the police and National Guard in the world, but you cannot use them if public sensibility will not tolerate a military presence.

I can remember Mr. George Wallace, who ran for national office from time to time in those days, saying something to the effect that he would bring peace and safety to America's city streets if he had to post a militiaman every hundred feet along the curb. New Yorkers ground their teeth in horror at this. The man obviously wanted to kill us all. He would shoot our children down in cold blood. No one seemed to conceive a picture of these militiamen interposing themselves between our children and the muggers and footpads who roam the streets of New York at will, year after year, terrorizing young and old alike, bludgeoning them and stabbing them, driving them cowering and scampering into their coverts like rats, interdicting all their parks and streets after sundown and generally getting what they want. Mr. Wallace had misread New Yorkers' minds at least: they prefer any filth, violence, and terror to a cleanliness, peace, and order that might in any way inconvenience anybody (the muggers, say) or might jeopardize the constitutional rights of anyone (the muggers, say) to pursue life, liberty, and happiness, which for these latter gentlemen means heroin, which in turn means my wallet, which in turn means my skull, or worse, the wallet and skull of some old woman returning home late to her tenement at 119th Street and Lexington.

(The line that the columnists adopted in the face of situations like this was that the way to end violence and disorder was to root out the causes of these disruptions. The fact that such measures might take centuries did not suggest itself to them, so they never told us what we were all supposed to do about getting knocked on the head while their measures turned us all into nice people.)

So we lived with the subway strike. I think it lasted for ten days. It gave us all time to reflect on the nature of public order. I had thought, naively, that there was an entity, "law", such that it could be invoked in any situation for the salvation of that situation. Not so. A young lawyer friend of mine from Cornell and Oxford, who had arrived in town that September and who worked at one of the most venerable firms in the city, pointed out to me with glacial equanimity that the law itself is subordinate to the pleasure of the people and that there are things you can't do even if they are legal. If the people hate the sight of the National Guard, then you can't bring on the guard (not to shoot the strikers but only to drive the buses). Those buses and subways were the sovereign province of the men who operated them, and nothing in heaven or on earth could violate that sovereignty: no mayor, no court, no militia, and no moral question about the interests of tcn million people.

The end of the strike came with the city granting the "package" that had been asked for and unanimous acclamation for the team of mediators who had worked tirelessly to bring about this settlement that was so equitable for all concerned. We never found out much about the people who had lost ten days' worth of their livelihood. They belong to a group, along with the victims of the muggers, that New Yorkers won't let you bring up in political discussions.

3

The Styx

Not long after this, the great blackout fell on the city.

It was just about dusk. I had come back to the apartment from my day at the university library down on Washington Square, and Lovelace and I were sitting having tea at the table in the living room. Our windows looked north over the whole city, with the Empire State Building dominating everything from its place twenty blocks up Fifth Avenue from us. I had put a record on the machine—the fifth Brandenburg Concerto, I think. As we sat there drinking our tea and chatting, we noticed that the music sagged a bit, as though someone had put his finger on the edge of the record and was slowing it down. Then the lamplight wavered. Fie, I thought: the building is having trouble with its power supply.

I think we had vaguely remarked about it to each other when, with elegant and silent finality, the entire city winked into blackness. My chair happened to be facing the window, and I had looked out just then to see if any other building was having trouble and saw the Empire State Building itself disappear.

When apocalypse falls on you like this, you find yourself wondering about the small things, in this case where the candles were, and whether we had any to begin with. The huge outlines of the situation don't present themselves to you right away. They never do. Blackout, marriage, earthquake, jubilee, the Huns—when these things sweep you up, you are likely to be thinking, "What have I done with my hanky?" or "Unless I tie my shoe here, I'm going to stumble."

We found some candles and lit one or two. But then what do you do? It was not as though we were in pain or danger and were being called upon to *do* anything. We did not have to flee. There was no one to rescue, as far as we knew. And it was clear enough what had happened, so we didn't have to rush about and find out what was going on. So there we sat.

In other circumstances it might have appeared that we had gone to some pains to achieve this idyll. Dusk, the tea things all set out nicely, candles, just the two of us. Who could ask a better setting for a tryst? But it is hard to shift into the tryst frame of mind when you have been bundled into it by circumstances this bizarre. No doubt lovers dream of caves, islands, and glens where they can be alone. But if they find themselves flung into these places by the vagaries of war or pestilence, the scenery turns out to be somehow less than what they had fancied.

Not that Lovelace and I minded for a moment finding ourselves thus tête-à-tête in the gloaming. It was just a question of being unable to experience it *as* a tête-à-tête in the gloaming. With world news like this having suddenly gaped open at your feet, you don't just as suddenly shut out the world, even though it is perfectly clear that there is not one single thing you can do about it.

Anyone who has ever had the electricity go off in a thunderstorm knows how it won't let you alone. You can't go three minutes without being plucked by the sleeve by the situation. You think, "Right. We'll settle in, wait it out, and enjoy ourselves." After a moment someone suggests making a cup of tea, since there's nothing else to do. That ought to be simple enough. Right: I'll just go plug the kettle in. *Plug the kettle in*! Ha ha ha! Aren't we the slaves to electricity now! So after a bit you think, "Well, let's make a piece of toast anyway, even if we can't have tea. That'd be nice: toast and butter here by candlelight." Toast! What, pray, do you propose to toast it in?

And so forth. You can't have soup, or make fudge, or look at kodachromes, or anything else.

We finished our tea (we could at least finish what we had). Then it struck us that the phones don't usually go dead when the electricity goes off, so we made a few phone calls. That validates things a bit, giving you a chance to exclaim and carry on over what a lark it all is, or what a debacle it all is. The point is that you can *go on* about it with somebody. And in this case, being the victims, as it were, we could adopt the cheery and heroic stance of "Oh, we're fine. There's not a thing to worry about. No, we don't need to be rescued. Yes, we've got sandwich stuff." We managed, I think, to get through via long distance to both sets of parents.

But then you start to think. Suppose this goes on. The food in the refrigerator will spoil. The water will fail as soon as the tank on the top of the building is empty since there will be no power in the pump to get more water up there. Then the city will begin to panic. People will want to get out. There will be traffic jams. Refugees. Frenzy. Violence. Streams of people with bundles running for the bridges. Ten million people making for the country. Should we, then, prudently slip out now before the panic sets in? We could get the car out of the garage downstairs and be across town and through the Lincoln Tunnel and away before everything falls apart.

But that seems a little alarmist. So you stay, trying to steer the tricky course between foolhardy alarmism and foolhardy unconcern.

We thought it would be fun to go out on the street for a bit, just to see what things were like out there. So we walked down the nineteen flights to the lobby, and out. The streets, of course, were not dark, since the headlights on the cars had not been extinguished. But there was the problem of traffic lights. What is everyone supposed to do at the corner of Fifth Avenue and Fourteenth Street, say, with no red and green lights to regulate things? Does Fifth Avenue decide, instantly and en masse, to be charitable to Fourteenth Street and let them pass? Even if we could get Fifth Avenue to do this, who is to give the signal to Fourteenth Street that their turn is up, and that it is now Fifth Avenue's turn to pass? One imagined jostling, all-night shouting matches among the drivers who had managed to reach the intersection, all demanding their rights, and earnest mediators trying to arbitrate among the parties, and still others snoring in pastoral cynicism at the wheel. Clearly, the electric impersonality of traffic lights covers a multitude of sins, I thought: it forces a pattern of charity on us all willy nilly. It *makes* us dance to the tune ("You First!") to which the saints in the City of God dance.

We walked down to the Village. Through the open doors of the bars and coffee houses, we could see silhouetted in candlelight the faces of the people who had either been caught there or come in to be neighborly and share the fun of the big gaffe. For that is what it was, obviously. There was a short-circuit somewhere. Somebody had thrown a wrong switch or something, and here we were. The mildly surprising thing to us all, aside from the sheer astonishment of finding out that the City could be steeped so suddenly in this stygian darkness, was that obviously all the current for the whole enterprise had to run through some bottleneck somewhere and that everything could be brought to a halt by one mistake. For all we knew, it might have been a rat on a routine foray who had blundered across some bit of copper somewhere and been frizzled to an instant clinker. There he was, unhappy creature, black and scorched, soldered to the circuit, a small ashen smudge like the ashes on Ash Wednesday, reminding us all of how contingent everything is. Remember, O City, that dark thou art, and into darkness thou shalt be plunged.

So here we were, millions of us, hailed with our contingency—not, one thought, the sort of reflection likely to attract much attention on an ordinary day at the height of the rush hour and the early evening scramble for home, theater, and assignations. Your average sidewalk evangelist with his sandwich board reminding us that The Day of the Lord is Near is held to be a fool. Now, suddenly, we are all obliged to pause. Heavens! We've been blithely assuming that all these lights were simply *there*. A given. One of the fixities. Our undoubted right. And suddenly the foundations are shaken.

It was like dying. The rat on the circuit (or whatever it was up there) was like a small tumor or a faulty valve in your heart. Yes, a faulty valve: it's quite easy to see what's wrong, and all we need to do is to open this up here and then—see! The blood flows once more. The electricity comes on. No problem. It was really rather simple.

The only difficulty is that the man is dead now. The city is dark.

Oh, well now, that's a different matter. That takes it quite out of my hands. I can make an incision, and I can clip back this skin here and saw through those bones there and show you what the little malfunction was. But of course it's gone beyond my purview now.

Yes, of course. We need embalming fluid now and cosmetics. We need long palls, drawn hearses, and the Requiem. Suddenly contingency is upon us, and we are at the Throne of Grace, beseeching and saying, "*Recordare, Jesu pie...*"

For most of us that night there was time enough to reflect on the oddity. This mighty city, the capital of the world, forced to stop like this by a small fluke somewhere. Most of us filled in the time with chat, drink, and sleep. (There was a great deal of waggery in newspaper columns during the next few days about how jammed the maternity wards were going to be nine months from that night. I think, as it turned out, there was a bulge in the statistics nine months later, but I may be making this up.) But for some thousands of people the situation was all too vividly like death. These were the ones crushed into elevators stuck between floors and into subways stuck between stations. These people had no elbow room in which to contemplate the ambiguities of contingent existence. Like dying people, they found themselves wholly occupied with the terrible physical conditions in which they found themselves. Here they were, squashed into multiple coffins, as it were, obliged to strive vainly for hours (the blackout went on for exactly twelve hours) in ghastly erotic proximity with horrible bodies they had never seen before, which they hadn't asked to meet, and which now sweated and heaved against them in this torrid and impotent struggle. Breasts, bellies, buttocks, armpits, wigs, bald heads, insteps, dentures, pimples, hair—a dionysian danse macabre, hour after heaving hour, one's eyeballs rolling in empty and hysterical hope, peering into the blackness, bereft of light. Jersey and denim and wool and orlon, all rumpled and sodden. Babies squalling, old men coughing thickly, fat women wheezing, everyone eventually being driven beyond patience and heroism to truculence, bestiality, and despair.

I come from a long line of people on my paternal grandmother's side who suffered from claustrophobia. They had been known to smash doors in their efforts to get enough air. My older brother, who was a varsity wrestler at college and did not himself suffer from this disorder, claimed that whatever hold he got me into, he could never keep my head from popping out of the tangle. I had to have air, broken neck or no. During the blackout, I conjured wild pictures, in vicarious agony, of these scenes in the elevators and subways. Hieronymous Bosch himself never imagined anything more elaborately infernal. The unusual luck that had got me home in time was a most gracious gesture from heaven in my behalf.

4

And Nonny for Woodstock

There were other events that excited the city during our years there. Besides the transit strike and the blackout, there were also a garbage strike (a "uniformed sanitation workers' strike"), a teachers' strike, and the student revolt.

The garbage strike was the most visible, and pungent, of the upheavals, of course. Even the chance tourist could not escape its effects. The sidewalks became like mountain paths, zigzagging between great drifts of rubbish. There were some areas of the city where the smell became almost unbearable, although in the neighborhood to which we had moved by the time the garbage troubles came, seventy blocks north of where we had begun, the maintenance men in each building were doing a heroic job of getting everything into enormous plastic bags so that there wasn't much question of smell.

Here again, the ordinary citizen was not sure just who was taking what view of it all. I never knew what to say, for example, to the handymen in our building, since, for all I knew, they were wholly in sympathy with the sanitation workers—a sort of blue-collar solidarity binding them together. However, it often seemed to be the case that people whose work was domestic as opposed to public service (butlers, maids, doormen, etc.) were scandalized by events like public strikes. Our doorman, for example, clucked and wagged his head over the garbage strike, but it was always discreet clucking, since he knew that the chic and affluent denizens at this Park Avenue address could be counted upon to support most sedulously any proletarian insurgency.

What nobody seemed to have an answer for was the question of the long view versus the short view in these crises. That is, you can settle *this* strike well enough, but what precedents for the future have you thereby established? The sanitation workers' case was irrefutable: Why should they be the ones, we all asked, to be nice and restrain themselves when the rest of the world was getting rich? And besides that, who is to decide that this sort of work is worth only $10,000 a year? (This was a decade ago: I am sure that that figure itself is laughable now.) Who is putting the price tag on various kinds of labor? Who says that brains, or family connections, are to be rewarded more lavishly than brawn? Let's just debate that now.

And of course nobody who must run for political office can afford to urge that one kind of work is worth less money than another. If there are enough voters in a given occupation, and if they can get themselves organized, they will be sure to have the solemn support of the candidates. For example, if there were an enormous voting bloc of oil tycoons, say, whose platform was that $500,000 a year is a hardship wage, we will find the people who need votes supporting the claim.

So the city is left debating wages for sanitation workers that stunt the salaries earned by people who have gone to school for sixteen or eighteen years in order to qualify for their job. The difficulty of anyone's talking about this topic with any candor would be illustrated by what I am doing right now. I am walking gingerly here because I know full well that at least half the people who read this paragraph are murmuring to themselves, "Oh-oh. A real capitalist here! An embryonic robber baron. Wants the workers trodden down and kept in their places. Well, it figures."

The trouble with this analysis is that it greatly overestimates my economic sophistication. I do not *know* the answer to the question. I find myself banging about like one of those bumper cars at an amusement park, lurching from anarchism to Jeffersonian democracy to republicanism to feudalism. (I would secretly like the last, let's face it, so long as I could be a royal duke. And, unlike my fellow dukes, I would be a good one. My thralls would love me.) It's not so much the question of garbage collecting's *not* being worth so many dollars as the other question of how societies are to go about setting price tags, especially in an epoch like our own, when there does not appear to be any agreed-upon system of calculating these things.

I keep wondering, for instance, about doctors. How have they got the jump on us like this, so that they can simultaneously ruin us all with their fees and treat us like naughty children to boot? That is, one is not allowed to talk to one's doctor as though he were a tradesman peddling his wares or his services. He's the adult and I'm the child when I'm in his office. But that's not how it is with the electrician or the plumber: *I'm* the big man there, and *they* have to be nice to *me* (although admittedly they, like the doctor, have me by the throat financially). How has this pecking order arisen? And actors: Who put the price tag on Elizabeth Taylor or John Wayne? My apprenticeship for my job was longer than theirs—What's going on?

And so on. Clearly, if I put it to the public with enough abrasiveness and enough organized support from my colleagues, assuming that there are enough of us to ruin an election or throttle a city, then who is going to say that my services (I teach English) aren't worth $85,000 a year? What answer is there to my case other than "That's absurd"? But try to put some teeth into your answer if I and my colleagues have a pistol at your head.

The garbagemen had such a pistol. It was simply that sooner or later New York would have to have its garbage collected. And the men knew that New Yorkers would prefer to drown in swill than call up the National Guard to collect it all. Everyone knew this, so the pretense of the city's negotiating with the garbagemen was a charade.

We were all apprehensive, not so much about the stunning "package" to be awarded to the garbagemen as of the birds circling around watching the situation. As soon as the garbagemen were paid off, we all knew that the police and the firemen, and every other group, would swoop in. And who could gainsay it? If I had been a New York policeman, thrust into the breach every day, no one would have persuaded me to look the other way while my brother city employees got paid $3,000 a year more than I did. And the firemen: their already perilous job became more and more daunting during those years as they found themselves pelted with rocks, bottles, and bricks when they answered alarms in various ghetto neighborhoods. (I never learned why the householders in a given area would want to drive away the very men who were coming to put out the fire, but then there were many vagaries attending life in New York that I never got to the bottom of.) Who is to say to these firemen that their services are worth only so much and no more?

What is the answer? The police and the firemen demanded matching packages. And the teachers followed suit before long.

Now teachers have been an underpaid crowd since the beginning. But with the tang of militancy in the air in New York, the public school teachers whiffed battle and liked the smell. A man called Shanker emerged as the teachers' champion. His case was not only that the teachers were underpaid for the job they were supposed to be doing (teaching), but that they had had another job loaded onto their shoulders without having bargained for it, namely, the job of keeping order in hell.

The tales that came out of the hallways and schoolyards of the public schools in New York were terrifying. My own assumption when I was a schoolboy was that absolute respect for all authority was axiomatic and that doom awaited me on the far side of any faintest trace of disobedience or disrespect on my part toward teachers. I can remember the sensation of my whole torso melting with terror on the few occasions when I had, in fact, got myself into trouble. The whole future collapsed. Perdition gaped. I was exposed for the fraud I was. Now I was to get my just deserts. My terror could not have been greater if I had gone to schools where they flogged miscreants. The very sight of the principal of my grammar school, for example, nearly turned me to vapor with sheer fright. She was a stocky woman named Miss Sayre, with gray bobbed hair (or at least it seems to be bobbed in my memory) and steel-rimmed pince-nez with a chain. She and I had never had any but the most amiable contacts, but when she would appear in the hall I would thrill with almost catatonic fright. She was, as far as I was concerned, Authority Incarnate, and there was no appeal from that serene court. Once when my sister and I were late for school (for some entirely satisfactory reason I am sure: no one in our family has ever been late for any appointment), we had to go to the principal's secretary, presumably simply to inform the office

that we had arrived. I swam the whole way. I might as well
have been a thousand fathoms under the sea. No damned
soul approaching Rhadamanthus on his throne ever felt greater
terror.

That was when I was in kindergarten, in the early 1940s.
Once when I was in seventh grade we were having a fire
drill. The rule was silence and order. The boy in back of me
took to treading on my heels, so I, in mock discomfiture,
capered along in a silly way for a few yards, escaping his
tread, as it were. It was typical of my efforts at evil: others
bring it off, while I never can. I get tickets if I speed up to
twenty-eight miles per hour in a twenty-five mile-per-hour
zone, while everyone else goes by at seventy. In any case, on
the morning of this fire drill, Miss Perkins, a redoubtable
and venerable teacher of geography and sponsor of the Mon-
itor Club, happened to be watching from the steps of the
school building. As we filed back into the building, I knew
that she was looking straight at me through her rimless pince-
nez. I tried frantically to look circumspect. But I heard her
fingers snap as I approached. It meant one thing: step out
here, Tommy Howard.

Shame, mortification, ruin. My ears burning, my world
in rubble, my guilty soul pilloried. That was nearly thirty
years ago. As I write this now, I am covered with anguish
and confusion. The sensation that suffuses my memory is the
one that overwhelmed me that day.

I had to appear before this Miss Perkins and sign a paper
saying that I had misbehaved. It went into my permanent
file, I was told. I assume it is there now, a blot forever on the
scutcheon.

It was from this viewpoint that I read in the papers about
what went on in the schools in New York. To me it was
unimaginable. That there could be a scheme of things pos-

sible in which students did *not* do what they were told was as inconceivable for me as a one-sided piece of paper. It was a contradiction.

And yet here was the contradiction in our laps. It became clearer and clearer that it was not only possible, but the order of the day in New York. The picture one got was of classrooms full of brigands abristle with lead pipes, brass knuckles, and stilettos, hulking in and out at will, manhandling the teachers, raping the girls, scorning the police who had been sent into the halls, flunking every test, and all the while making an enormous profit pushing grass and acid.

The notion not only that there was no order, but that no order was possible, blew my categories once more into shards. By moving to New York I had clearly moved into a place, and into a scheme of things, quite different from what I had supposed the world to be like. I once wrote a book about how big and exciting "the world" seemed to me as I emerged into adulthood. Travel, people, theater—all that. But what seemed to be happening now was that I was being obliged to watch the mortar in the foundations of civilization dissolve away. There were *not* the recourses I had supposed there were. There were *no* barbicans between us and the Huns. There were no axioms, no suppositions that remained at the base of the fabric. I raged. I panted in terror. I gesticulated.

But my New York friends looked at my frenzy with weary and urbane amusement. The poor child. Straight out of the woods. All these ideas he's got. Times change, dear boy. Nothing is given. It is possible to jettison everything.

And so the teachers' strike went on. Their demands, like those of the garbagemen, were not to be gainsaid. The questions were unanswerable. Except of course that New York found the answer it always finds: pay.

But meanwhile there were the children out in the streets. It crossed my mind once or twice that the taxpayers ought to organize themselves and refuse to pay a penny to the city as long as any widespread public breakdown was afoot. Or, perhaps more fairly, subtract on a remorselessly accurate accounting every hour's worth of inconvenience they had suffered as a result of the breakdown: so many days' worth of garbage piling up, so many days' worth of schooling denied their children, and so forth. But the mountainous organizing and the bookkeeping demanded by such an undertaking would daunt the pluckiest spirits, and the taxpayers are not renowned for pluck. Indeed, it is necessary that they lack pluck, since if modern society is not to break down altogether, you have to have one element that can always be counted on to give way. You can't have the irresistible force of higher wage demands meeting the immovable object of truculent taxpayers. It is part of the vocation of the taxpayer to pay on demand.

So with their children playing hide and seek among the trash cans (or worse: What dreamer supposes that *that* is what goes on among the trash cans?), they had to pay for the schoolwork their children weren't getting.

And, one wondered, what sort of picture was being built up in the imagination of these hundreds of thousands of children as to the nature of human society and existence? They were witnessing a scheme of things not only where nothing was sacrosanct, but where nothing had any value at all. Whereas all civilizations and societies have guarded their institutions with taboos and strictures of one sort or another, New York was out to show history that you can keep things going without those primitive aids. Damn restrictions. The judge can drrrop dead in his black rrrobes. We are modern. We are free. We are franchised. We will contest every point.

Demands will defeat any authority. Litigation will topple any institution.

The children of New York observed this, and they liked what they saw. Their schoolteachers, made impotent as far as disciplining the students went, turned their frustrated energies on the school boards and commissions that had emasculated them. And the parents, softened up by two generations' worth of psychiatric counsel on how not to damage children's self-determination, were interested not so much in keeping alive in their children any notions of order as in guaranteeing that the inalienable rights of all parties were preserved intact. What the eighteenth-century fathers never anticipated was the situation where irreconcilable demands met each other head on, with both parties denying the authority of the arbitrator. With judges being admonished to drop dead and teachers being pummelled out of classrooms and parents being told to get lost and mediation panels being snorted into oblivion by rank and file workers, what sort of order is one to conceive in one's imagination?

None, clearly. Order itself became the villian finally, since there was nothing else left to blame for everyone's troubles. Children had problems, we were told, because their parents and teachers overbore them with authority, and parents had problems because Western society had overborne them with authority, and Western society had problems because somebody back there (the Puritans? the Catholic Church? the Jewish prophets? God?) had overborne it with authority. All of us, from God on down, seem bent on using our authority to force some pet order of our own on everyone under us.

So ran the argument. When trouble flamed anywhere in New York, the question asked was not "What exactly is at stake here on the long view?" but rather "Right. How shall we dismantle everything and start over?" The assumption in the imagination of New Yorkers is that established order is a Bad Thing.

Over against this, of course, New Yorkers are not prepared to set anything so stark as chaos. Chaos, they suspect, is a word thrown up in self-defense by feudal barons and other obstructionists. Over against order we may set the free, innocent play of self-determination. If we could only bring this about, all the terrible weight of institutions and laws and conventions that brutalize us all would be lifted, and we would caper out together onto the lawns of Elysium. New York would be Fun City.

And, suddenly, Elysium was enacted before our eyes. In 1968, in the middle of New York's agon, we had the spectacle unveiled. All at once, the children—or their older brothers and sisters, actually—broke free, ran into the country, and showed us the alternative. No use arguing about it. A picture is worth a thousand words.

And so they gave us the picture, in living color, at Woodstock. A quarter of a million of them gathered to celebrate freedom and to inaugurate the new aeon. Complexity and sin and sorrow and pain and endurance—all the burdens under which humanity has tottered for so many aeons—were left behind. Behold. The Day of the Child was at hand. Now was the accepted time. Now was the Day of Salvation. Woodstock was anointed to preach liberty to the captives and to set at liberty those who were bound. Woodstock, without suffering any passion, and without descending into hell, would lead captivity captive. In one huge puff, death and hell were overcome. Behold, the City of Peace is with Man.

Not, mind you, Imperial Salem. Oh, no: that is a city foursquare, with adamantine foundations and a King on a sapphire throne. A vision, if there ever was one, of tyranny and repression. Ah, no. Woodstock is builded as a city that is unstructured. As the trampled litter is round about Woodstock, so Aquarius is round about those who fear him. At Woodstock, we saw the reefer high and lifted up, and the smoke filled the temple. There we saw the bride, clothed in cutoff denim, with her breasts fondled by all her lovers. There we saw the souls of the satyrs calling out from under the altar for more hallucinations. Bring to the feast not timbral and trumpet and high-sounding cymbal, but electronic bass and electronic bass and more electronic bass. Raise the decibel count. Hosanna! Raise it higher! Bump, O ye kindreds of the earth! Grind, O ye young men and—um—maidens. Rise, crowned with light, emancipated Woodstock, rise! I was glad when they said unto me, Let us go into the house of the Flower People.

For one weekend the feast went on. The astonishing thing was not so much that a quarter of a million children should gather for such a donnybrook as that the press—the civilized, more-than-blasé New York press, which ritually congratulated itself on the clarity and unsentimentality of its outlook—should attach itself to this spectacle, like any draggled camp follower, solemnly telling us that the "kids" were showing us a new way. Hear, O ye jaded suburbanites; hear, O ye robber baron landlords, ye Wall Street brokers, ye uptight middle-class Wasps: the kids are showing us a new way—the way of love. Behold how they love one another.

It was as though no one had ever heard of this oddity called love. It had never been proclaimed in our history before. There had never been an epiphany of love for us to see. Simplicity and self-giving, and purity had never been incarnate and enacted for us. There had been no train of martyrs and confessors and virgins and widows anywhere who exhibited in their poured-out lives, century after century, what this love might look like. No one had ever come across a single Sister of Saint Vincent de Paul, with her obscure life of Rosaries and bedpans, who lived and prayed for the life of the world. No one had ever seen the people in the Salvation Army shelter taking in whatever blew in off the streets and feeding it and giving it a bed. No one had ever met a schoolteacher whose obscure life shuttling between her classroom and her tidy flat had for its only reward the occasional sight of some pupil coming alive to what she was saying. Nor had anyone, apparently, ever seen so much as a painting of Sebastian, pierced with arrows, or a Virgin Mother pierced with five sorrows, or a young Nazarene pierced in hands and feet and side—all of them for the sake of this love that, we were told, was being unveiled for the first time at Woodstock.

But what did it look like there? The only piercing anyone heard about there was the piercing of the mainlining needles of ecstasy—not, one would have thought, to be placed in a reliquary along with the Nails and the Spear.

As the press gasped in hope and awe over the weekend at Woodstock, the thought struck me that we might perhaps give this huge epiphany of love the chance to prove itself by encircling it with a chain-link fence to keep out bourgeois exploiters and allowing these quarter of a million children of love to demonstrate for us all just what not only a weekend, but a year, of love looked like. One year. We want to see what a society conceived thus looks like, not just a picnic.

There would, of course, be one or two things that somebody inside the fence there would have to decide upon. Latrines, for example. What about latrines? You can't have one huge latrine covering the entire area for everyone's random convenience. Some specific places will have to be picked. Right. Let's have one here, and one here, and one there. No—I want one over here. Oh, no—that's right where I have spread my blanket. Well, move your blanket, brother, 'cause I'm digging a latrine there. Oh, no, you're not. Hey, you two—remember, it's love all the way. Smile on your brother. Well, I'll smile on him just as soon as he moves his damned blanket. Now wait . . .

Whom shall we vest with the authority to decide this quarrel? Authority? Are you kidding? What do you think we're doing out here anyway? Authority is one of the bourgeois things we ran away from when we came out here. No way. Well, then, let's call an ad hoc committee of the whole. Hey, everybody, gather around. We're going to rap about this latrine here. Who's *she*, telling us all to gather around? We've just got this weed started here, so we're not going to any caucus.

But once they did get the holes dug somewhere, somebody would discover presently that holes fill up. Hey, what we need is a drainage system. That way we won't be forever digging new holes. A *system*? Are you kidding? Systems are what we ran away from when we came out here, baby. No systems. Yes, but we've got to do something about all this sewage. I mean, it accumulates. Oh, well, then, build a bloody system if you have to, but don't hassle me about it. Right. Whom shall we send, and who will dig for us?

I will. I'll get some of the brothers and sisters to dig trenches and lay culverts. Hey, c'mon, we're all going to dig.

Dig, dig, dig. I'm going to knock off. It's hot out here. Hey, no, you can't. The trench isn't even ten feet long. Screw the trench. I'm not going to work all day while the rest of these mothers lie around smoking. Let some of them do it now.

And then somebody shows up sick. Vomiting, eh? Here, take a drink of this—it'll cure anything. What is it? Hey, this is nothing but some cheap Mexican wine. It's burning my stomach out! I need help! Somebody help me! I'm dying! Here, put this around your neck. What is it? It's a guinea pig's foot. Damn you and your guinea pig's foot. Somebody get me to a doctor. A *doctor*! Are you kidding? Those guys are just another part of the establishment. Here—a little sex'll fix you up in a hurry. Oops, she really is sick. Hey, somebody—

And then it starts to rain. Hey. Those guys up there have got all the good spaces under those oak trees. We're moving our blankets up there. Oh, no, you don't. We got here first, and this is our turf. C'mon, brothers—make room for the brothers. Brothers, hell—if you had gotten here first you wouldn't want us coming in on top of you and crowding you out. No way, baby. This patch is for *these* brothers.

And then somebody runs out of food. Hey, man, share some of your bread with us. Hey, man, this has got to last us another week. Can't do it. Sorry. Hey, man, we're hungry. Share the bread with us. Kiss off, baby, this bread's ours.

And so forth. Municipal problems. Labor-management problems. Production and distribution problems. Property problems. Pollution problems. Rights. Authority. Systems. Caucuses to talk things through, with everyone shouting to be heard. Then somebody with the loudest voice and the biggest biceps bellowing for order. His brothers lining up beside him to back him up. A putsch. A junta. Then order. Courts. Advocates. Judges. Penalties (no pot for six hours for you, baby). Somebody discovered selling grass at a profit. Aha! A Mafia, eh! Gouging the brothers and sisters! So much for you, man.

Woodstock a year later. A ruling elite (it is called the establishment outside). Managers (we called them fat cats back then). A police force (we called them pigs when we came here last year). The guillotine (we've got to keep order *somehow*).

The mayor, the blackout, the subways, the garbage, the teachers, the kids. What city is this? What city? Pray for the peace of New York.

5

Vulgarity Unmasked

One of the things you do when you live in New York is shop, or at least go to the shops. When it turns out that you can spend eighty dollars for four neckties in three minutes, you begin to adopt a guarded frame of mind as you set out.

Lovelace's favorite haunts were Altman's, Lord & Taylor, and Bloomingdale's. The tiny boutiques, the salons that the public has never heard of, where the very rich get their shirts made and watch haute couture paraded on slinky and emaciated models—we vaguely knew these places were there, but never seemed to need the wares they offered. There was a small shop called "A La Vieille Russie" at the corner of Fifty-Ninth Street and Fifth Avenue. I used to look across at it from the steps of the Plaza Hotel, where we would find ourselves for dinner now and again, and wonder what they sold in there. I had the impression that they sold nothing but coronets, and perhaps Fabergé eggs. Not, in any event, what one needed right at the moment. And there were places like Harry Winston and Cartier, where you peered through armored glass at emerald necklaces and ruby brooches in the shape of cockatoos, or Steuben Glass, where you could get crystal porpoises or polar bears for your coffee table at $13,000. Gucci, just a few doors down Fifth Avenue from all this, sold suede handbags and luggage with Gucci's very own red-and-green fabric strip around every piece, for tremendous sums of money, and there were innumerable nooks in Bonwit Teller (Hermes, Turnbull Asser, Bill Blass, and Braggi) where you could buy a scarf or a cake of soap for seventy-five dollars. I was never sure just who the customers were. I used to wander through these places looking as soigné as I could, and I had the impression everyone else was doing exactly the same thing. The great thing was to appear lithe, breezy, and beautiful, as though you had just blown in from your townhouse and were in quite a rush to get out to East Hampton before the guests arrived, and you had to pick up some little thing for so and so, she's such a love.

Or else you were getting garden furniture for the terrace you had just fixed up on the fortieth floor. In which case you went to Bloomingdale's furniture department, if you didn't have your own decorator to find things for you on Third Avenue. I always had the overwhelming feeling that the people who were actually buying things there were the heavy suburban couples who prowled among the reclining leather chairs and day beds, whereas the rest of the crowd swishing around and around had come precisely to swish around and around. There were very, very few women there sometimes. Lots of little silk neck scarves and Cardin shoes and twenty-eight-inch waists, but no women.

Lovelace, as I say, went to Altman's and Lord & Taylor and Bloomingdale's. She knew where to look for things and what to buy. For her, shopping was neither the fatuous business of merely presenting oneself expansively, all chic and beautiful, in the stores and boulevards nor the gluttonous business of amassing all the diverting wares one happened across. If I, in contrast, had been sent abroad into the streets to find things for the apartment, we would have ended up with a clotted and dizzying assemblage of rugs, sconces, trumeaux, lavabos, credenzas, armoires, ottomans, cane, wicker, wrought iron, distressed walnut, knots, tiebacks, tassels, swags, valences, brocade, palms, ferns, Florentine boxes, and busts. She knew exactly the look she wanted in the apartment, and she went after that. Unlike me, she knew she wasn't furnishing Le Petit Trianon or Blenheim. Her reason for not buying a given item was not that it wasn't *pretty*. Rather, it was that *we* didn't need it. It took me some time to arrive at this chaste approach to things, and now, even after eleven years of living with her, my inclination is still to snap up, or dream of snapping up, any villa, chateau, or gewgaw that is for sale, provided, of course, that it is very beautiful and very fine.

She was, as a matter of fact, chic and beautiful when she set out shopping. In those days women still wore gloves, and even hats, when they went to the stores in midtown. She had a fawn-colored suede Robin Hood hat that she wore, and when she would appear with this on and gloves, and her tailored coat and Capezio boots with the tiny heels, I would wonder how I had gotten up the derring-do to ask this gamine to marry me. Once when I was waiting for her in front of the elevators at the Plaza (her parents stayed there on their visits to the city), the golden doors opened, and in the sumptuous crowd of important-looking people who stepped out there was an especially lovely lady. "Ah", I thought. "Now look at that one. Some very happy man will find her one of these days." It was Lovelace. I always felt very fine walking through the Plaza lobby, or into church, or along Fifth Avenue, with her on my arm.

The whole business of buying and selling comes at you violently when you live in a place like New York. It assails you in all sorts of ways. There are little, pale, shaven-headed, teenage Hare Krishna boys swaddled in saffron sheets trying to sell you a magazine for a dollar to help you achieve serenity. There are unsteady old men in bogus sea-captain hats in Times Square, trying to dragoon you for a boat ride around Manhattan. There are men selling pretzels and chestnuts from little carts in the gutter, and nice women at Bergdorf who show you peignoirs in mirrored, carpeted, beige-and-pink salons. There are burly men with cigars in upstairs lofts who sell you mattresses and umbrellas, and the men who sit in the Madison Avenue galleries, for whom the possibility of your buying one of the paintings on display appears to be a matter of the most sublime irrelevance. And behind all this, of course, there must exist the world where property and bonds and oil and nations are bought and sold over telephones and around enormous polished tables.

Who started the business of buying and selling? Cain? Enoch? How do you learn how to do it? What sort of research is it that lies behind the shape and color of packaging, for example, and behind the displays in a given store? Who found out that the word "Exxon" would sell more gas than the word "Esso"? Or that Eastern Airlines needed to repaint its planes in white with a black-and-blue stripe down the length of the fuselage and up the tail at an angle? Who knows that you should put the handbags and costume jewelry at the Lexington Avenue entrance to Bloomingdale's, from which most of the women arrive, and that you can put the cosmetics up half a flight, after they have gotten properly into the store? Or that the men's store should be on the Third Avenue side? Do more men come in from Third Avenue than from Lexington? Or is it that the women would lose heart if they had to walk the whole way through the store before arriving at their section? Who found out that we will all buy Crest toothpaste in that zippy white tube with the green streak on it and that the old orange-and-yellow zigzag of

Kolynos (or was it Ipana) won't attract people in the 1970s? How does Aramis know that that dark brown packaging will make men buy those toiletries? And who is on the committee that decided that bright yellow flasks in odd shapes will sell scents and unguents to other men?

Who decides that toughness will sell a product (Marlboro); or filmy shimmer (Modess); or short, choppy sentences (Volkswagen); or awkwardness (Benson and Hedges)? Somebody back there in the marketing research rooms must know a lot about us. They do, too. It works flawlessly. What are we?

Have we all jumped across some line drawn by the advertisers? When Potiphar's cook went out to get vegetables and fruit for dinner, was he regaled with claims about how garden fresh and Sunkist they all were? When Prince Igor's housekeeper needed soap for the royal doublets and hose, did she have to fight her way through a tussle of claims about how snowy and gleaming it would all come out? When Dr. Johnson wanted coffee in Will's Coffee House, did he have to endure a song about how some planter went up and down the rows in Colombia turning over every leaf to find only the best beans for Dr. Johnson's cup?

What's going on? Is this city serious or not? If a sudden apocalyptic horn were to blare out over the city, calling all the plain and good people to line up over here, and all the humbugs, frauds, mountebanks, popinjays, imposters, and gulls to line up over there, which line would be longer? Where would I be? Alack. I believe all this trumpery. I believe it when a shop names itself Elegantissimo. I believe the decor of Henri Bendel, which proclaims with every square inch "Smart". I believe the tall, thin, pencil sketches in the *Times* that show me how worldly and lithe I will look if I buy those trousers. I believe the ambience in Hammacher

Schlemmer that says "make sure he knows you bought his present here".

Lovelace never seemed prey to this hoodwinkery. She knew where to go, and she knew what she wanted. But she also knew what she did not want and, more than that, what she did not need. She knew the difference between appropriateness and ostentation. Three cheers for everything that is beautiful and fitting and a pestilence on all that is tacky and tawdry. But we do not need to snuffle and forage through every shop in the city like pigs under a truffle hedge, rooting up and gobbling everything that looks nice.

Part of the difference between Lovelace and me in this connection may be attributed to the fact that she is a woman and I am a man. That, of course, would appear to be gratuitous insight, except that nowadays loud, articulate, and unhappy women shout at us in every journal and talk show that there is no difference between the sexes. There is, though. And I am not the one who thought it up, nor are they the ones who will erase it.

One of the differences, surely, is that, despite what everyone has always said about women being gullible and easily preyed upon, there is something wise in a great woman's intuition (which word itself has been cheapened by a lot of tiresome cant), which gives her a glimpse, hidden to men, of the Center. Perhaps a truly womanly and free woman knows who she is and what the world is, much more naturally and directly than a man does. I am not speaking here of silly women. I married one who was not silly and hence found myself obliged to reckon with the Center. I had been drawn, as it were, not by any skein thrown out by the guiles and wiles of a *belle dame sans merci*, but rather by the cords that draw a man in toward the precincts of felicity. And they are cords given in the ordinary course of things to women to spin, I think. A man's natural inclination seems to be to scour round the marches on the borders of those precincts, stoutly establishing a claim for himself by conquering kingdoms, seizing chairmanships, solving riddles, or writing books. He is, perhaps, profoundly aware that he is only on the perimeter. It has indeed been given to him to protect that perimeter; but there is a Center that he looks for, and probes for, with fierce desire and sorrow, but that he cannot find unless it is opened to him. It is the woman who knows where that Center is. Indeed, she is there. Indeed, it may be said that she *is* that Center, in a mystery. It is not for nothing that human imagination has seen the figure of the goddess there, in maternal fecundity, at the Center. Nor is it for nothing that in the Story in which all those other stories are gathered up and find their fruition, we find the Mother, full of grace, highly exalted, made the God bearer. Left to themselves, the men are solitary, frustrated, sterile, and vicious.

For a man may make havoc of his role as protector and conquistador. He may become a brigand, plundering and raping terrain that is not his. But for him to inherit the land rightly, the gate must be opened to him. He must be invited to come in and reign by the one who has been there all along and who herself awaits in virginal solitude the coming of the King who will plough and irrigate the land that it may fructify.

Arrant nonsense? Of course. Vegetable myths. Corn gods. Earth mothers. It has all long since been disproved.

But then what *was* it all about? Is it true, what they tell us now, that the difference between men and women is no difference at all? Or at the most only an irritating and unfair obstetric division of labor in which some malign evolution, set afoot no doubt by some murderously clever protohistoric male caucus, loaded all the boredom and burden bearing on the women? The mystery-cult notion of womanhood, with its intuitions and its breasts and its womb—ha! And the notion that women know something that men have to struggle to find—ha! And the idea of women being there at the place that men must seek—ha! The very diagram of the body itself, with soft, moist canals leading to secret fallow regions waiting in fecund potentiality for the great vessels bringing the fructifying rain—stop, stop, stop! It's all too embarrassing. It's embarrassing for all of us: for us Victorians because the whole business is too dreadful to begin with and for us moderns because it's too primitive and naive.

Very well, then. It doesn't mean anything. The body is not a diagram of anything. Nothing means anything after all. The eyes aren't the windows of the soul. Your beloved's neck is not an ivory tower, nor his belly like a cluster of pomegranates. Her breasts are not like bunches of grapes from the hills of Lebanon, nor her hair like the gold of Ophir. The Canticle had it wrong. The poets had it wrong. The priests had it wrong. The savages had it wrong. The androgynes and lesbians have at last preached to the spirits in prison. They have led us at last out to the bald, scientific truth about these mysteries, which are no mysteries after all. It is all a plot, all a cheat, all dust thrown in our eyes by the villains.

But if it is a plot and a cheat, then, I thought, it is an infinitely more splendid and blissful cheat than the reality they are telling us about now. It is the drama of the man coming to the woman and finding there the image of what his whole being seeks, and of the two of them enacting together the blissful inequalities of love, and discovering the paradoxes that defy the pettifogging efforts of the revisers to equalize everything and gauge narrowly who's getting the bigger slice of the pie—paradoxes in which, as in any dance, it is the very leading and following that both partners find to be liberating.

But that is a long distance from the shops in New York. The connection, it began very slowly to dawn on me, is that Lovelace, being a truly free woman, knew where she dwelt (although I am not sure she would say that she knew she knew) and hence did not need to snap up every bibelot. For her, the appeals addressed by advertising and shop displays—appeals that I found so enthralling—were not irresistible. She admired whatever was truly lovely (fabrics, furniture, knick-knacks), but she did not have to have it.

6

Of Marrows in Cream

Eating in restaurants is a major preoccupation in New York. I do not mean having your lunch hour at Chock Full O' Nuts: I mean "dining out".

The business of dining out soon enough runs into money, and one finds that unless one has limitless funds to put into this sort of thing, it can't be done very often. After we moved uptown, away from our little $2.50 fettucini places, we did not do much dining out on our own.

There were a great number of times, however, when we were taken to dinner. When you know that your host and hostess look on the business of eating in the best restaurants the way other people look on bowling or movies (that is, as an entirely happy way to spend the evening and the money), then you can settle in and have your dinner with zest.

There were some extremely splashy places to eat in those days in New York. There still are, I am told, but it may be a different set of places. My list is ten years old now. The names you softly let fall back then were Le Pavillon, The Colony, The Four Seasons, Lutêce, La Caravelle, La Seine, La Grenouille, Voisin, The 21 Club, La Côte Basque, and a few others. You didn't come at it head on. That is, you didn't say, "We—ah—went to the Pavillion last night." You said, "The marrows in hot cream and paprika at The Four Seasons are really quite astounding", hoping against hope that whoever you are talking to had caught *where* the marrows were being served and had gotten it clear that you had been eating there.

We went to these places quite blithely unaware of the terrible nuances that float in the air at important French restaurants. The table where you are put, for example: It was not until I read later in some magazine about that tortuous and finely tuned world that I guessed the awful truth: we had consistently been seated at what everyone else in these places knew to be the most humiliating tables. The maître d's, all attentiveness and courtesy, had led us, in effect, to dunce stools, I am sure. It was all right in our case, since we had nothing particular to prove to anyone and didn't know about it all in any event, and maître d's must know that it is impossible to insult people like us who have clear, innocent, amiable eyes. They must know, from the instant you put your foot on the threshold—indeed, from the timbre of your voice and your accent when you ring earlier in the day to book the table—just what they are dealing with. If you are both important and civilized, they activate treatment number 1. If you are highly cultivated but not very important, you get number 2; if you are quite important but a boor, you get number 3; and if you are neither civilized nor important but only a spendthrift, you get number 4. We may well have gotten number 5, that is, the alternative reserved for people who defy their categories. I strongly suspect that this is what happened at one of these places at lunch one day. We must have looked harmless, which is a disaster. We were put at an altogether unsuitable table out in the stream of waiter traffic and left unattended and hungry for long, dismal periods. At the end, they charged our hostesses $125 (four people, no drinks, no dessert . . . and this was 1969) and let us find our own way out.

Nuances like this must be insupportable for people who know and care what is going on. No wonder people rage at head waiters and sweep out calling down pestilence on their heads. If, in the nineteenth century, to be "cut" by some grand matron was the ultimate obloquy, perhaps in New York now it is to be scorned by the head waiter and his men in full view of everyone. It did vaguely flit through my mind once or twice in those days that our table was not getting quite the agile and sycophantic attention that some of the tables around us were commanding, but I attributed my suspicions either to my imagination or to the fact that I am a marked man and that every waiter and doorman and clerk in the world chuckles to himself when he sees me coming. I was once eating with some friends in a restaurant in Stuttgart, and the waiter brought everyone else's food, then made me wait for exactly forty minutes for mine (and it was not a souffle, or a chateaubriand either, noted on the menu as requiring forty extra minutes). Another time in Madrid I finally, at 3:00 A.M., had to stand up, wave my arms, and call angrily and loudly to get the check. Admittedly dinner had begun at midnight, but back then I thought that three hours was long enough to have spent at table, especially at that time of night. As I remember it, I was having dinner with two Arabs, and they were bemused by my haste.

But we were, as I say, entirely unaware of the darker side of the French restaurants. It was great fun to anticipate an evening at one of these places. Very often we would meet our host and hostess at the Palm Court for something to drink before going on to dinner. This was, by all odds, the splashiest place in New York, if by that you mean the combination of extravagant decor, lots of coming and going, and the sense of sitting at the hub of things. There are quiet places and private clubs, of course, that are infinitely more posh and there are numberless places that are noisier and brassier. But the Palm Court has achieved just the right ambience for everyone who wants to be elegantly on display in an atmosphere that no one can sniff at.

It is in the Plaza, for a start, and that is a very long head start. There you are, on the nicest piece of real estate in Manhattan, bang at the corner of Fifty-Ninth and Fifth Avenue overlooking the Park. Whoever designed the Plaza deserves the gratitude of us all. Suppose the architect had put up a terrible monolith such as Hilton builds or as one sees in Miami Beach? What a loss it would have been. But no. There sits the Plaza, like an archduchess, presiding graciously from under her steep green roof and pointed corner turrets. You sweep up, or rather, slam up in a cab, to one of the great canopies—there is one on the Fifty-Ninth Street side across from the Park, and one on the Fifth Avenue side opposite the Pulitzer Fountain. The doormen are there, to be sure, but you are given, faintly but ever so unmistakably, to believe that there are more important people just behind you. Limousines mean next to nothing here, since any boor can hire one of these long, black Cadillacs for the evening, so it is not your arriving in a taxi rather than a limousine that betrays you as unimportant to the doormen. They know.

The canopy itself is heated in winter with dozens of red-hot electric heating rods reflected down onto the sidewalk by shiny metal concave plates, and there are great canvas curtains gathered back from the canopy to the facade of the hotel. (This device has been picked up by most motels and suburban steak houses and combined with javelins, red knobbly-glass lamps, heavy dark grainy wood, and bogus heraldry to give you the feeling of stepping into something ancient. It miscarries in those places.) You go up carpeted steps past great standing lamps that look like gigantic candelabra.

Once I saw Eartha Kitt helping a small child up these steps and put out my hand to help, but she scorched me with a glance of scorn and fury. People like Elizabeth Taylor and the Rolling Stones stay at the Plaza, and you see them from time to time. They seem to book into vast suites on the fifteenth floor and do all their receiving and entertaining up there, so you don't see them very often. There is likely to be a sheikh or a sultan up there somewhere as well, but I never saw any. There are old women who live there in rooms that they have inhabited, one hears, for fifty and more years and whom you can see now and again sitting on the enormous brocaded Empire chairs in front of the gold elevators or in little loveseats opposite the Palm Court.

To get from the main entrance on Fifty-Ninth Street to the Palm Court, you go around the great bank of gold elevator doors, past the newsstand and the gold house phones, and follow the corridor that circumambulates the Court itself until you come to the opening where the maître d' is. The Palm Court is really a sort of square space within a bigger square space, cordoned off by huge planters full of palms, with gold and glass wainscoting running around the whole perimeter. You are, in effect, sitting in a carpeted garden.

This maître d' was named Joseph, and we got to know him, as it were. To this day I believe that he meant it when he acted glad to see us come. If it was part of his job as host at the Palm Court to appear delighted to see us, then that external necessity of his job had somehow percolated down into his heart, and he really did find some sort of pleasure in seeing his familiar customers arrive. I do not think he was a fraud.

He or one of his lieutenants would show us to one of the little marble tables. The chairs were all bright green brocade. The arrangement *under* the tables was ambiguous, and one could never find a place for one's knees and feet. Different sorts of things were served here at different hours of the day. You could get breakfast, and brunch, and tea, and drinks, and late evening dessert, which meant all kinds of fancy gateaux and parfaits and sticky confections from the trolley. There were usually pink tablecloths, but at the cocktail hour the marble tables were bare, I seem to recall.

In the hour before dinner, which is usually when we found ourselves there, they had a violin and piano going, played by two men who were perhaps from Hungary or Austria, one thought. They played "Dr. Zhivago" and "Raindrops Keep Fallin' on my Head" and "On the Street Where You Live"— that sort of thing. Everyone clapped, and the two men bowed extravagantly. The note struck in these exchanges was a kind of mutual courtesy and delight, as though to say, "Ah. It's such a lovely time we're all having here, and those were wonderful tunes you played, and all the people are so wonderfully civilized, aren't they?!"

I used to look around to see who might be there. Angela Lansbury was there once, in an ivory-colored suit, and blinked appreciatively at my obvious recognition of her, I think. Once there were two men at a table next to us whom I decided to believe were Aaron Copland and Virgil Thompson. Nearly everyone there was from Central Europe, as far as one could tell, but there were occasional stunning black models being taken for drinks by, I assumed, photographers and agents and people like that.

The important thing about the Palm Court, of course, was simply that you were *there*. The occasion was everything. A glass of Campari or a dry roasted cashew tastes the same everywhere. But the fact that you were sitting in this bower right here was the whole point. The combination of being *in touch* while being at the same time safely hedged about with palms and candelabra and doormen: that is what one wants in New York. The pleasures of Eden and the pleasures of the City simultaneously. Lots of people, but no unimportant ones. Lots of chatter and clink and tinkle, but no banging of tailgates and garbage can lids. All is well.

After an hour or so at the Palm Court you went on to dinner. Actually, it gave you a very leisurely feeling indeed if, instead of going *out*, which meant doormen again (tips) and another taxi (more tips) and traffic and noise and then yet another doorman and a hat check person at your destination, you just trod around the lobby here in the Plaza to the Edwardian Room or the Oak Room.

What shall I have tonight? I nearly always ended up ordering smoked salmon to start with. I liked those thin, cold, wet slabs with the capers scattered across them. Shrimp or lobster one could get anywhere, and a dozen blue points or littlenecks on a plate of ice was something, along with escargots, that I never could rise to. And Beluga caviar was $15 per nibble. The Strasbourg pâté and terrine de foie gras generally turned out to be not exactly what one had looked for. In a few places you could get something completely different—for example, the marrows in hot cream at the Four Seasons or somewhere.

After the hors d'oeuvres comes the soup. Vichyssoise? Green turtle? Onion? In the early days of all this dining I thought you could have a rich hor d'oeuvres *and* a rich soup, having of course eaten a whole dish of cashews at the Palm Court, and still approach your entree. You can't. I found myself wilting in my chair before the fish or the meat ever came along. I finally learned to have either some salmon *or* some soup, and if soup, to have something austere like jellied Madrilene. I was not enough of a bon vivant to row through course after course of heavy cream sauces, and soups, and dressings, with crackly rolls, butter, and profiterole or eclairs into the bargain, like some apple-cheeked eighteenth-century English country squire. I ought to have taken a lesson from the Princess Dragomiroff, who, in the dining car on the Orient Express (which film I saw, alas, only several years later), ordered for her dinner "a poached sole and one potato".

The wine steward presents, in one way, the most delicate set of negotiations, since, short of one's having been brought up in a chateau, one's approach to the wine list is likely to be mostly humbug. One has a few little wines that one likes. I had discovered Bernkastler Doktor by trying it out after coming across it in a short story by Isak Dinesen. But as far as really knowing anything about vintages or being able to tell the difference between one vineyard and another, much less about whether it has all been cellared properly or decanted properly or allowed to breathe for long enough—how many New Yorkers, or even Frenchmen, know what they are talking about? I am sure bravado plays a major role in it all.

There was a most amiable young Belgian wine steward, first at the Pavillon and then at the Colony. I would get him on my side by murmuring a few offhand remarks in my Belgian French accent (I was taken for a Belgian once in France by a Frenchman, which flushed me with euphoria), hoping against hope that he wouldn't sail off into a long and rapid monologue, forcing me to confess that I couldn't follow him. Then I'd look knowingly up and down the list. I knew a few sticky wines to avoid, and one didn't ordinarily want rosé, and German and Italian wines are not what one usually looks for in these places, and the Château Mouton Rothschild was $145 per bottle. I sometimes roused enough candor to ask him what he thought would be nice, and he never failed us. What I did not know, of course, was whether he was thinking to himself, "Ah. Let's have a bit of fun here. I'll bring

out a bottle of stale vinegar and watch them go on over it."
He may still be chuckling.

I had never gotten a very clear picture as to what one is to
do with the cork that they put down ceremoniously in front
of you. Is one to roll it under one's nose between thumb and
forefinger like a cigar? Peer at it narrowly? Taste it? Ignore
it? Nod knowingly? I am still not sure.

7

Enter Mr. Eliot

But it was not all opera and strikes and shopping and dining. We had come to New York in the first place for my graduate studies at New York University. I always had a shaky view of this, since the *terminus ad quem* for such studies is, ordinarily, a doctoral degree. But I supposed that a doctoral degree was almost impossible to get and that one had to be pertinacious, resourceful, intrepid, and brilliant if one were ever to think of having one of these cachets. Since I knew myself to be none of these, I took the view that sooner or later the truth of the situation would come to light and that I would be rusticated. No doubt I would get a crisp note from the university authorities telling me that I might want to consider finding my identity along lines other than advanced academic lines. But meanwhile I plowed along, tacking toward the inevitable day of shipwreck.

One of the first reefs you have to negotiate is the foreign language examination. Most universities require (or did, during my era) two, and the German examination was before me. I had sat for the French a year or two earlier at the University of Illinois, where I had floundered through to the master of arts degree. Many universities let you come to these examinations with a dictionary, the idea being that you have learned your language, but that anyone might come across a word here and there that he doesn't know, even in his native language, and what is the harm in his looking it up. At New York University, however, they take a different view. No dictionary may be brought, which means that you must arrive having mastered thousands upon thousands of vocabulary words.

I had gone to Tübingen for the summer a year before this to learn German in a crash course and had, in a desultory way, picked up a good bit of the language. But as far as being able to read a piece of literary criticism in German, which is what they ask you to do in these examinations, I was far from prepared. So I bought one of those boxes of vocabulary cards that you see in bookstores, and for weeks during September and October got out of bed *de bonne heure*, so to speak, in order to batter lists of words into my memory. This is the worst possible way of learning a language, of course, since the words come at you in a vacuum and you have to depend upon frantic mnemonic devices to help you remember the difference between *gekommen* and *bekommen*, and *wer* (which does *not* mean "where") and *wo* (which does not mean "who" or "woe" or "whoa"). Once in a while there is a gratifying one like *der Gummischuh* which cries out for mnemonic horseplay (it means just what you think it does: gummy shoe, that is, overshoe). But the German prepositions like *auf*, which may be followed by either the dative or the accusative case, thereby raising the terrible question of *den* versus *dem*, will elude all but the most ferociously Teutonic imaginations.

I passed the examination. The worst preliminary barriers were behind me now, since I had also passed, besides the French examination, the requirement in Old English at the University of Illinois. The Old English requirement is by far the most daunting part of one's graduate career in English. I used to wish that you were allowed to call it "Anglo-Saxon": that made it sound more impressive. If you say "Old English", lay people think you are talking about expressions like "hey nonny" and "ye olde wool shoppe" and fail to appreciate your achievement. But scholars call it Old English, not Anglo-Saxon, and it is a language infinitely harder than German or Greek to master, since most of the words occur only once or twice in all of the literature of Old English, and hence there is not much in the way of a body of common words with which you can get familiar. Oh, to be sure, there are words for "go" and "grip" and "kill" that occur again and again—everyone in the poems did a lot of going and gripping and killing. And there are the words that look like their modern English descendants such as *ic* ("I") and *ceosan* ("choose"). There are numberless words for "man", including *wig* and *athel* and *guma* and *tulk*.

And then there is a worse difficulty in that the language keeps changing. The poems that you study are scattered over several centuries and come from several different areas of England. This is much more complicated than our saying, for example, that yesterday we read a poem written in Lowell, Massachusetts, in 1850, and today we read one written in Nahunta, Georgia, in 1950. In Anglo-Saxon times (it is all right to refer to the period, or the people, thus: just don't call the *language* Anglo-Saxon) England was carved up into seven little kingdoms, and nobody took any interest in what we might call communication facilitation. So that your struggle to master the forms of a word that shows up in some seventh-century Northumbrian tale by no means guarantees that you will be able to recognize the same word when it shows up in eighth-century Wessex or ninth-century Kent.

And, to make matters worse, there are seven *classes* of verbs, each class with its own vagaries and oddities. And the word order in the poetry is to syntax what the Labyrinth was to a straight road. I struggled with Grimm's Law (a set of observations on how certain Indo-European consonant sounds change as they muddled on into Primitive Germanic) and with Verner's Law (exceptions to Grimm). Everything seemed subject to metathesis, which looked unhappily like metastasis to me. Whenever I come back to Old English now, I have to begin all over again. It is all I can do to read Genesis 1:1 ("On anginne gesceop God heofenan and eorthan"), let alone *Beowulf* ("Hwaet, we Gardena in geardagum, theodcyninga thryn gefrunon").

The graduate faculty at New York University seemed to be made up entirely of luminaries whose names one saw scattered all over the publications of the scholarly world. It is a high and august world in which renown means not that you will find cordons and flashbulbs besetting your path the way Senator Kennedy or rock singers do, or that passersby will catch their breath upon realizing that they have seen you as one does with Greta Garbo (I did see her once, on Sixth Avenue: I am sure it was she), or Truman Capote. Rather it means that at a scholarly conclave some graduate zealot will come up to you and thank you in an urbane sort of way for the clarification you provided on the variant readings of that line in Aelfric's *Colloquy* in your article in the *Journal of English and Germanic Philology*. You win fame by publishing things like this. Unless you can think up an idea for a popular textbook, you do not ordinarily get riches into the bargain, since the scholarly journals pay little or nothing, the idea there being that you should really be paying *them*, since their publishing of your article provides a major shove to your career.

One of the courses that I took was a course in Middle English poetry taught by a man who had made a number of phonograph recordings of poetry read in Middle English, which was the language spoken in England during the later Middle Ages after the French of William the Conqueror and his barons began to percolate down through the Saxon speech of the natives. Chaucer wrote in Middle English, although he did not know it was middle. It is much easier to read than Old English. Almost everyone can muddle along in Chaucer. For example, in "Whan that Aprill with his shoures soote", that "soote" might be taken for "soot", whereas it really means "sweet". But it does not take long to get going in Middle English.

The name of this course was "The Alliterative Revival", which referred not to some Pentecostal awakening among the peasantry in which they all began to speak in alliterating sentences, but rather to an odd outcropping in the late fourteenth century of *Old* English poetry, whose main feature was not rhyme but rather alliteration. The lines tended to look like this: "Sithen the sege and the assaut was sesed at Troye." I began to read these poems under this man's tutelage. One of his specialties was reading aloud in class. It was an intoxicating business. That poetry comes at you like an incantation or a spell. Up and down, on and on, mellifluous or husky, strumming or clashing, dulcet or braying. The sounds matter. It concerned the poet whether he was filling up his line with s's or with m's. We sat in that class and were lulled and roused by the sound of the professor's voice moving through those lines. We read about King Arthur, and about Sir Gawain and the Green Knight, and about the pearl.

The poem about the pearl is a lament. A man has lost his "precious pearl withouten spot", which seems to mean his little daughter. He falls into a sleep, which nearly every Middle

English poet tended to do at the beginning of his poem, and has a vision. He finds himself standing by a brook on the far side of which is a fair and immaculate maiden—his precious pearl withouten spot. He wants to leap across and recover her straight away, but she will have none of it. Instead, she taxes him with hard questions about his motives (which turn out to be almost entirely selfish) and gives him a long, arduous discourse on the blisses of heaven and the holiness demanded of its citizens. She herself turns out to be one of the brides in the great procession going to the nuptials of the Lamb. The poet wakens and returns to his solitary life, chastened, but with the vision of holiness and bliss having been vouchsafed to him.

I was reading all of this as true, of course. That is, the poet's picture of heaven and of the people who, because of their snowy purity, are able to experience the heavenly splendor as not boredom but bliss—this was true. That old poet had not cobbled it all up out of his private fancy. It is what Christians believe. It is what the Church teaches. It is the Christian vision. It was odd, running into all of this there in that late-afternoon classroom on Washington Square, with scholarship more than holiness in the air.

But that was it, really: vision. The kind of sight that pierces beyond clutter and murk and sees things in their stark clarity. Dreams that suddenly become awesome in their clarity and truth are called visions. The things that the saints see in their moments of unblurred sight are called visions. (Seers and poets and saints have always been the ones who see farther into things, or through things, than the rest of us, who muddle along with the dust of mere appearance clogging our eyes.)

The old poet's vision was true, I thought. Naturally the class discussions did not run along that line; but we were

assuredly confronted in that classroom with a vision attested
to by crowds of good people, poets or plowmen, down
through the centuries. The way across the brook to the thing
he wanted more than anything in the world was a long one.
His pearl had no authority to invite him to hop across all in
a minute. He had to turn and go back to his work, relin-
quishing his demand for his pearl, nay, even his search for his
pearl; and he had to learn, through long, sorrowful years of
fidelity to his work below, to want the thing beyond the
pearl, the thing that was itself the joy of the pearl and all her
maiden companions in the bridal procession of heaven.

If one does not believe all that, of course, the poem is still
a very charming monument to late medieval sensibility. I
never found out how my colleagues understood it all, but it
did seem to me that we were ourselves being vouchsafed a
glimpse of things that, if they lay beyond what we would see
when we walked out into Washington Square, were nonetheless more important by far than what we might encounter out there. If what the poet had told us was mere quaint
fancy, it was nonetheless fancy more splendid by far than the
charade one found everyone staggering about in out there in
the Square. Somehow, from the sordid matrix of medieval
life he had been able to fashion this vision of bliss, whereas
we, surfeited with luxuries beyond anything he had ever seen,
are unable to come up with anything much more sublime
than a truculent poetic howl.

The big entree in this course was another fourteenth-
century poem called *The Vision of William Concerning Piers the
Plowman*. Most people call it simply *Piers Plowman*. You had
to buy two fat volumes for this poem, one containing parallel texts of the three versions of the poem (the poet could
not let it alone: he tinkered with it for years), and the other
full of footnotes and other scholarly apparatus. It was a

daunting business to approach these tomes, and one thought, "We're in for it now. Here's where we run aground in our graduate studies." The editor of the work was a man called Skeat who lived in the nineteenth century. He holds a place in the calendar of scholars not unlike that held in the Christian calendar by, say, Hugo of Saint Victor or Saint Frideswide. Laymen have never heard of Skeat, but those who know have, and they bow accordingly. And with good reason: the work that Skeat did on that poem, pulling it all together and arranging it so neatly for us, and collecting all that information about it—it all warrants any canonization that the scholarly world can bestow.

But Skeat did not write the poem, of course. Nobody knows who did, actually. The best conjecture is that someone called William Langland did, but you cannot find out much about him. The main thing that happened to him, according to his poem, is that he fell asleep on a May morning in the Malvern hills and had a vision.

What he saw was a *fair field full of folk* (he was writing during the alliterative revival). All the people in the field were running about, some doing their work, and some malingering. There were tradesmen calling out their wares ("Hot pies! Hot!") and winners and wasters of every sort. There were lawyers who truckled and pettifogged, and priests who trafficked in the holy things.

At one end of the field stands the Tower of Saint Truth. Into this rout eventually comes Piers Plowman and tells everyone that he can show them the way to the dwelling of Truth. A number fall in with this idea, and off goes the ragtag on its sudden and devout quest. But it does not last, as one might have guessed, and before long everything has fallen apart, with all the people back to their sins of simony, lechery, gluttony, avarice, wrath, and all the other deadly sins.

Langland's story is not easy to follow for the simple reason that he has much, much more on his mind than he can pack into any conceivable narrative. Before he has finished with his story, for example, Piers has turned up first as a plowman, then as Saint Peter, then as Christ himself. The pilgrimage to find Truth never succeeds, and neither do Piers' efforts to get people to do their work properly. But you are whisked up into a poetic vision of things that leaves you thunderstruck. You have long since ceased to complain that you can't follow Langland's story. For you have seen Everything, as it were. You have seen a whole tapestry of the fourteenth century, and you recognize it all too well, alas. You have seen crowds of common men and women rushing hither and thither with neither a very clear idea as to what they are doing nor any very stout resolve to do it if they were to find out. You have seen the predators that grow fat by sucking the life of the rabble, and you have seen holy souls who want to do something about it. You have seen allegorical figures (Lust, and Anger, and Holicherch, and Lady Mead) pace across the stage all mixed in with real flesh-and-blood people. You have seen the Passion of Christ and the harrowing of hell in lines of such startling nobility that you wonder how anyone can ever find those events dull. And you have seen the figures of Do-wel, Do-bet, and Do-best, who, in the utter simplicity and straightforwardness of their names, disarm you completely and make you wonder whether the subtle and epicene characters that undulate through modern stories are not laboriously insignificant.

What we were talking about in that classroom once more were sin and salvation. We talked about manuscripts and about editors and about allusions and literary conventions and about the rules of poetry. But what were staring us in the face all the while were sin and salvation. Langland, like his hero Piers, was clearly most zealously opposed to sin and most anxious that we all be saved. Here we sat, a roomful of urban jades, who had got way beyond the naïve topics that concerned Langland. For us the important thing was to have finely honed sensibilities and discriminating tastes. Ah, Langland: so quaint, so observant of his era, so inventive. They thought of things so fetchingly in the Middle Ages. Life was so manageable. The universe was so tidy. You could classify human actions and attitudes into such nice categories. Sin and virtue. Sin was to be deprecated, and virtue commended. You were responsible for what you did, and therefore you stood in danger of hell if you ignored your responsibility. What a fascinating worldview! What fun to do one's doctoral research on Langland.

There is no "campus life" at New York University. The graduates and undergraduates alike find their extramural divertissements along the streets of Greenwich Village, and there is no end of variety there. It is not an area, however, designed to underscore and nourish any ideas you may have picked up in your graduate reading of Middle English poetry about holiness.

Holiness. There was the crunch, perhaps. One suspected that holiness alone, eventually, was the state of affairs in which a man could find the freedom and bliss that we all seek so assiduously. The streets of the Village were there, and the shops in midtown, and the opera and New York's politics, and everything else. Good and bad all mixed in together. Beautiful things and tawdry things. The sublime and the bestial. The austere and the licentious. Renunciation and surfeit. Salvation and damnation. Invitations to heaven and to hell.

And then it was upon me again, in yet another graduate course. This time we were far from the quaint world of the

Middle Ages. In fact, we were squarely in our own world, the world of the modern city and its denizens. We were reading the poetry of Mr. T. S. Eliot.

In that poetry you move along a track that takes you all the way from whorehouses past fatuous and chic parties where the people move about talking about Michelangelo, and slum alleys where you can smell cooking, and bleak upstairs rooms with tattered window blinds, right on through to the tiny church of Little Gidding, where a man named Nicholar Ferrar once made the attempt to order common life in such a way that the plain duties and rhythms of household life would find their natural fulfillment in the offering of the Blessed Sacrament. Hey, nonny! Here they were again: holiness, vision, immensity, arching over one and peering at one in those classrooms and reading rooms on Washington Square.

Eliot is implacable. He presses and presses his "overwhelming question" on you, and insofar as you dodge behind a feeble "Oh, do not ask, What is it?" you, like the faceless speaker in one of the poems, may be damned to the realm of twittering, hollow inanity. Or at least so the poetry would seem to suggest.

I felt as though I were being crowded along toward a bliss that I wanted less than anything in the world. After all . . .

8

"I Said to David Rockefeller..."

Presently I finished my courses, and we moved uptown. I thought it would be an idea to get a teaching job, but since I had never had a course in educational methods and hence lacked the official certification one needs in order to teach in the public schools, I applied to several private boys' schools. I was hired by one of them and found myself enchanted by what I found.

To any passerby, the school is just another doorway. But one of the things one learns in New York is that this difference is very much of the essence. The unassuming look, either in clothes or in entrances, may hide enormous eminence. The clubs, for example: they hide behind plain, unmarked doorways, while the gaudy emporia in Times Square hail their clientele with all manner of noisome devices.

The headmaster invited Lovelace and me around to his apartment for tea with him and his wife to talk about the job. He was your fantasy—your good fantasy—of a headmaster: graying, twinkly eyed, old school, Oxford educated. Lovelace liked them both immensely, and that is always a factor in one's decisions, since, like litmus paper, Lovelace turns blue in the presence of any sort of fraud or humbug, so I trusted her response to this man. It was an altogether well-placed trust, as it happened.

I was given a classroom full of eleven-year-old boys who turned out to be exceptionally bright. They also turned out to be the sons of people who were terribly eminent in one way or another. It was all very exciting. Here was the son of the most famous television newscaster in the world, and here was the grandson of a former U.S. President. One boy, who came from perhaps the most purely gold-plated family of them all, arrived at school one morning complaining that his mother had eaten most of the five pounds of caviar that he had been given as a birthday present. I wondered what solace I could offer in his hour of trouble. He was, by the way, utterly unspoiled, as were most of the boys there. I found that their parents managed to instill in their sons a modest and virtuous sense of value in things. These would be the men who would, later on, refuse to buy something, not because they did not have the money but because it was not worth the money. There was nothing flamboyant or ostentatious about their world. Very few of them appeared to have been coddled. This boy, for example, did not conclude that the world *owed* him five pounds of caviar.

I was impressed with the messages that would come up to my desk from the switchboard downstairs. There would be instructions about what time so and so was to be at the front door to leave for the weekend skiing, or what changes had occurred in so and so's dancing lessons. Once I was asked to tell Stephen A. that his mother's chauffeur would be at the door at such and such a time rather than the usual time. (His *mother's* chauffeur, I thought; heaven only knows what skullduggery his *father's* chauffeur may be up to.) Another boy arrived back from Christmas holiday with a deep tan. "Where did you get that?" I asked him. "Fiji." His father owned one of the fastest racing yachts in the world, and the boy had been with him on some race in the South Pacific.

Amusing things came out during lessons from time to time. Once in a geography or history lesson we were talking about the nineteenth-century expansion westward of the United States and of the enormous part played in this by the great railroad empires. One of the railroads was mentioned by name, and I heard a boy murmur, "That was my grandfather" (or great-grandfather—I have forgotten the generations involved). Of course it was your grandfather, I thought. Who else? Another time the presidential scion had to be excused for a few days because they were unveiling a portrait of *his* grandfather in the White House. It was all very heady, but if the boys were amusing, my colleagues on the faculty were even more so.

The relationship of schoolmasters to boys from very old or very rich or very famous families is an intriguing business. I suppose it is not unlike that of tutors and nurses and governesses: there is an intimacy that proceeds upon the perfectly clear knowledge on the part of all concerned that you belong to two different worlds. He will go on to another of the great schools; then to one of the two or three universities; then into a world of friends, responsibilities, inheritances, and assumptions that is not open to outsiders; you will go—where? Well, nowhere, for most schoolmasters. Year after year you will teach generation after generation of these handsome and blithe young princes and heirs apparent, but they will all move on, and the masters will seldom see a single one of them again, unless the boy is spirited enough to return once in a while for the old-boys' dinner.

My colleagues at this school were a particolored assortment. Most of them were frightfully civilized and were indistinguishable at parties and dinners from the fathers. They could talk knowledgably about London and Paris and Rome and Prague, and they sailed and skiied, and they knew

everyone and could talk about painters and orchestra con-
ductors and everything else.

The one whom I was replacing, for example (he had to
go off to the National Guard), was the sort of fellow that the
Appalachian Mountain Club used to field as hutmasters in
the White Mountains. Clear, ruddy complexion; blue eyes;
sandy hair; chunky torso; legs covered with blond hair—you
could see them in the mid 1950s playing touch football around
their fraternity houses in the fall. Then there was a blurred
young man who came in for a few hours every day to teach
French. He was thin and amiable and pale and came from a
very suitable Philadelphia family and had, as I remember it,
arcane interests (something like Egyptology or spelunking
or haute cuisine). Another man on the staff was a very tall
sort of horse who looked as though he had cartilege instead
of bone holding him together. He was a Rumanian, or at
least was married to one. He taught woodworking to the
boys, but was far too preoccupied with the job of making
things out of wood to keep order in the shop. He appeared
to assume that boys would address themselves to their drills
and lathes with some singleness of purpose if he left them
alone, so when I would go down to the shop to collect my
boys from him, I found myself caught into a melee of racing,
shouting, bits of wood, tools, glue smells, and sawdust, all
whirling together in a great din.

There were a few women on the staff. Besides the junior
school teachers, one of whom was known to us all as the
Wicked Witch of the West and another of whom was a breezy,
bosomy socialite herself who owned surely the biggest Saint
Bernard dog in New York, there were some adjunct women
who kept us amused. There was a small Austrian woman
who helped the slow boys with their reading. She and her
husband were gourmets and gave very small, very intimate,

very elegant dinners with many wines. She would tell us about these affairs in the staff room the next morning over coffee. She always knew what was going on under the surface in the school and looked out at us all with her beady, knowledgeable eyes.

There was a startling woman who came in two or three days a week. She had been retained by the school for the single purpose of, as far as I could see, regaling the boys by reading stories to them and by getting them to read out loud and write stories of their own. Her specialty seemed to be a certain ebullience, which, it was hoped, would communicate itself to the boys, thereby rousing them from their torpor and spurring them on to write stories full of derring-do. She stood about six feet tall, and except for her hair, which was an indeterminate yellow, she looked very much like the Nutcracker. I never was able to run down just how it was she put her lipstick on, but there was something odd about the arrangement.

Then there was a great, galloping woman who taught one of the sections of first grade. She and I discovered in each other a similar zest for certain kinds of phraseology and kept up an intermittent persiflage when we would encounter one another in the hallways. Her class was always the best-behaved one in the school. One could see the little mites creeping solemnly along to lunch or art or music, right in line. At prayers in the morning, that class alone in the whole school knelt bolt upright like a row of tiny Anglicans. Everyone else struck vague and tortuous positions. The theory was that we knelt, but a visitor might have mistaken the assembled worshippers for a hall full of young seals or a throng of yogis. This woman and I once sang Gilbert and Sullivan's "The Flowers That Bloom in the Spring, Tra-La" as a duet in an all-school musical program.

The head of the middle school was a saturnine bachelor who shook hands with each of his boys each morning by extending his little finger and hooking their extended little finger and who led his file of boys through the halls and up and down the stairs by holding the leading boy's necktie in his hand out front like a horse's halter. He glared balefully at them from his rheumy eyes, but they all adored him and called him "Clunko". He was an excellent cook and had Lovelace and me for dinner more than once at his apartment.

There was a heavy person who was built like an oriole's nest who taught science. He was entirely humorless and managed to keep the rest of us in a rage at him with his sententious solemnity.

The two men on the top floor who taught the two sections of eighth grade were both named David. They both spoke French fluently and often spoke it to the boys. History and art and music and languages were very much in the air up there. The one David always seemed to have stepped out of a men's boutique, fresh every morning. He wore well-pressed glen plaid suits rather than the tweeds and baggy twills affected by the rest of us. He was a martinet about music and, at prayers, would glower and puff if the boys took a breath in a hymn at the end of a line where there was no comma (for example, "the fields awake to cry NO BREATH DAMMIT their blessings on the Lord of Life"). The other David was English and had a hyphenated name. He had a shock of snow-white hair and wore half-moon reading glasses. The headmaster would have him read the Psalm at Friday morning assembly from time to time because he was so dramatic and articulate. Being, as far as I ever knew, a nonreligious person himself, this David always managed to deliver a magnificent reading of the passage while at the same time suggesting, ever so faintly, that *he* wasn't praising the Lord or calling upon *us* to make known his deeds. The implication was "this is what it *says* here, and I can give it a jolly good reading if that is what you want".

My two closest friends on the faculty were both characters out of an Evelyn Waugh novel. The one taught Latin and history and had adopted an attitude of weary ennui toward the world and life. He went about the halls with his head tilted up and lolling languidly to one side. His name was in the New York *Social Register*, a book that, until I began teaching at this school, I had always thought to be semimythical. These volumes, published yearly, lay about on desks and tables at the school, presumably so that we could all find out just whom we were dealing with in the case of a boy' parents. I heard one of my colleagues on the phone one morning speaking to the mother of one of the boys. "Good morning, Princess!" was how he began. He was not being funny. She was a Russian princess. There were a number of parents like that—White Russian exiles from the Revolution. Once Lovelace and I were invited to come to the Orthodox Easter festivities at the apartment of one of these families. They greeted each other with a kiss and "Christ is risen!" (in Russian) and tossed down innumerable tiny glasses of vodka.

The other of the Waugh characters I would see passing through the halls with a lordly hangover, dressed in Savile Row suits and soft leather pumps, with a wet, nonfilter cigarette pasted to his lower lip. I can't remember how we eventually met—it was by no means a given conclusion that one got to know everyone on the staff and far from given that one got to know this man. But somehow an acquaintance began. It was a dry, amused, oblique sort of business, with both of us murmuring arch comments about this and that. He knew everyone of importance and would spend his holidays in places like Addis Ababa, or Fez, or aboard somebody's yacht in the Aegean.

From time to time Lovelace and I would be invited to dinner at a boy's house. This was always very exhilarating, since we knew that we would be spending the evening with a picked company in a splendid house or apartment over excellent food and drink unimpeachably served. Once the father of one of my boys was away, and, it being his birthday, his mother had asked him whom he would like to have as a substitute. He picked me, so off we went to dinner there. We sat, the four of us, in a tiny study before dinner; then, when dinner was announced, we moved through the dining room to an alcove overlooking the East River. Maurice, the chef, had prepared some special souffles and sauces for the occasion, and we were very festive and intimate.

We went twice to dinner with the parents of the boy whose caviar had been eaten up. They lived in a house in the East Sixties. We sat in down-upholstered chairs and loveseats before an open fire. After dinner, which was downstairs from this room, there were cigars and cognac for the men around the table while the women went off to a sitting room somewhere to talk. The hostess, who was the mother who had eaten the caviar, was making some point during the conversation at dinner, in the course of which she said, "I said to David Rockefeller the other night, '*David* . . .' " The thing to do here is not to blink. She was not namedropping, and one has got to manage one's responses accordingly.

9

Heaven and Hell under Every Bush

Several months before we moved from Fourteenth Street I had begun to work at my dissertation. I had chosen a writer named Charles Williams for my research. No one had ever heard of him, or, if one had, it was a matter of his having seen his name in a footnote somewhere. He was a man who had worked as an editor at the Oxford University Press and who wrote novels, poetry, drama, criticism, and theology. A friend of mine had sent me one of his books years before, when I was in the army, and I had been riveted by this man's work.

Because he was such a minor figure from the literary viewpoint, the university library had almost no material on him, so I was obliged to go every day to the New York Public Library at Forty-Second Street.

The reading room there stretches, an immeasurable vista from end to end, lined with bookshelves that reach to the sky, it seems, and furnished with dark, polished wood tables and lamps that throw little pools of golden light on the table surfaces. There are usually a number of tramps sitting at these tables dozing over their newspapers. I began reading everything I could find on Williams.

I found that I was being summoned into a world as I sat there reading Williams. It was as though you were being beckoned through a gate and then led along ways that wound deeper and deeper into a landscape. But the odd thing was that the further you got into the new world, the more familiar everything looked. The way the guide talked about things was new, and he chose his words from a vocabulary you hadn't heard before. But he was talking about things you *had* heard about before. This that he was pointing out, and that, and that—had you not been here?

But the air seemed extraordinarily clear here. Everything seemed starker. Things stood out with a glory you hadn't noticed. Ordinary things that you had walked past for years were suffused with a light that seemed not so much to shed itself on them as to elicit from them some illumination already lying inside them. The clumps of trees, the houses, the hedges, the fences—you knew this neighborhood, but it was as though you had been until now a man almost blind or a man rushing by with preoccupations. You had missed most of it somehow.

But to represent Williams' landscape as rural is to misrepresent. He wrote about the city mainly—the city of London and, descried through the smoke and hurly-burly of this modern city, the City of God. Busy ordinariness clatters about you in his works, but somehow it ends up describing a pattern. The broken fragments of glass keep falling into place in the kaleidoscope as the circle turns. There is a center. There is a circumference. A hand turns it. The pieces—ordinary people's cluttered experiences—are beckoned, beckoned, into a pattern. The center holds.

What happens in most of Williams' stories is that things are going along in their usual rather pointless way for somebody when all of a sudden some *thing* crops up: the Holy Grail, say, or a pack of Tarot cards. Bang. The illusion that things are manageable and predictable is suddenly stripped away. Everything is up for grabs, so to speak, and now everyone has to mind his steps very carefully because what he does now suddenly turns out to be contributing to his salvation or his damnation. All heaven and all hell gape upon him.

If it sounds farfetched, that would be Williams' point: things *are* farfetched, if by that you mean that what lies about us is fetched from afar. Ordinariness opens out onto Everything. What I do, for example, at 11:25 A.M. on this Wednesday here in the library at Forty-Second Street and Fifth Avenue is helping me on toward becoming either a monster or a saint. All of my attitudes and acts find their native air in either hell or heaven. If I cut into a ticket line, muscling others out of the way so I can be sure of getting a ticket, that is hell, for it says Me First. If I throw down my gum wrapper on the sidewalk, that is hell, for it says, I do not care about the rest of you: it's convenient for me and that is all that matters. If, however, I give way to someone, or pick up a gum wrapper, that is heaven, for it says, Here: somebody has been messing things up. Let me just put it to rights.

On this view, the smallest courtesy is a tiny picture, or case in point, of the mightiest drama of all, the Cross. For in both of them the same principle is at work: my life laid down for yours. Exchange. Substitution. You first.

Ordinariness suddenly opening out onto Everything. Heaven and hell under every bush. That is how Williams saw things. The eye with which he looked at ordinary things was like the eye of a lover looking at his lady. The lover sees this plain woman crowned with the light of heaven. She walks in beauty. Her eyes are windows of paradise to him. Her body, every inch of it, is an incarnation and epiphany of celestial grace. In her he finds the ecstatic vision that his heart has sought.

All this passionate intensity, Williams would argue, is not illusion. The ecstatic vision of beauty thus vouchsafed to that lover is true, not false. The lady *is* as glorious as he sees her to be. It has been given to him, the man who loves her, to see the truth about her. The rest of us bystanders, mercifully, have not had our eyes thus opened, else we would all go mad. It would be an intolerable burden of glory if we all saw, unveiled, the splendor of all other creatures all the time. Our eyes are dimmed, as it were, for our own equanimity and protection. We cannot bear very much reality, said Eliot, Williams' friend.

For Williams, not just the spectacle of his beloved, but every rag, every moment, every tag end of every situation, every eyelash and event and happenstance, were full of the potentiality of glory. Heaven and earth are full of the majesty of thy glory, says the *Te Deum*, and Williams thought this was literally true. What we find in the ordinary routines of daily life is made of the same stuff as the highest mysteries.

For this reason, Williams could reach off after some remote and arcane thing and drop it into the middle of his story about plain, modern people. What he wanted to show was that, no matter who you are or what your station in life is, or what century you happen to find yourself in, you are taking part in the only drama there is or has ever been, namely, the drama of good versus evil, or of heaven versus hell; and this drama shows itself in plain acts of courtesy and duty well done *and* in mighty mysteries like the Passion and Crucifixion.

So, for example, in one of his novels he has a pack of the ancient fortune-telling cards, the Tarot pack, show up. One of the pictures on those cards is of a Hanged Man. Who thought to put that in there? Who knows? But it is there, along with a lot of other pictures of mysterious things like the Juggler, and the Fool, and the High Priestess, and the Lovers, and Justice, and so forth. But Williams does not lead us off into these remote mysteries in his story. Instead, no matter what notes sound from those remote realms, he keeps his story right here in the ordinary light of day, and before the story is finished, we see one of the main characters, a fussy, selfish, testy old bachelor who began the story by complaining about how everybody was forever intruding on his tranquillity—we see him go out into a wild blizzard at the risk of his life to see if he can help his sister, who is out there. And not long after this, in a scuffle which he has entered against his own self-preserving instincts, he finds himself turned upside down—in the very position of the Hanged Man on the Tarot cards.

The Hanged Man? Who was he? Nobody knows, but he seems to be perhaps a sacrificial figure. He is perhaps hanging there *for* somebody. Ah. Sacrifice. Yes, to be sure. That has always been more or less the focal point for religions, especially mystery religions, hasn't it?

Yes, it has. And if it means anything at all, it invites our participation. Oh, we may not end by hanging upside down, but we may have to get up from our pipe and slippers and fireside and just pop out into the blizzard to see if she is all right. We may have to hold that door open so he can get through with those packages there. We may have to get up at night to answer an infant's wail so our spouse can get a bit of sleep.

Sacrifices? Not very demanding ones, but sacrifices nonetheless, if only the offerings of a moment of time for the sake of someone else's convenience.

As I worked away at all of this in the New York Public Library, I found it pressing in upon me from two directions. On the one hand, I had to keep my academic feet on the ground. The graduate English faculty of New York University were not looking for ecstatic candidates. You had to show that what you were doing constituted a contribution to scholarship. The trick here is to say your piece in as turgid and polysyllabic a style as possible and thus regale everyone with the sheer weight of your work. Even if you have chosen to tabulate the number of times Anthony Trollope uses the word "vicar", you need to show that English scholarship has been working at a terrible disadvantage up to now for having lacked this information.

My job, as it turned out, was to try to show how these odd novels that Williams wrote might deserve a place in the shelves of serious literature rather than in the shelves with the ghost stories. That was several years ago now. My dissertation is there, bound, in the shelves with the dissertations. I have not noted any great surge among English scholars toward Williams yet, but things do take time.

Pressing in upon me from the other direction was the growing awareness that the world around *me* was beginning to be touched—gilded—with this Williamsian light. Plain ordinariness began to look more and more important. It was easy enough, living in that city, to suppose that the *extra*ordinary was necessary to one's happiness—the chicness and opulence and variety and fascination of it all. But what about the plain things that I shared with all men everywhere? What about the business that goes on, age after age, whether one is an emperor, a clerk, or a serf, of doing one's work with integrity, and of being trustworthy and generous and courteous, and of filling the office of husband, and then father perhaps, as it ought to be filled? On that accounting, it doesn't much matter whether you live uptown in New York or downtown in Bemidji or outside the walls of Nizhni-Novgorod: you have the same set of things to do.

How was I to see it all? Here I was, approaching middle age. For a decade of my adult life I had fancied myself a bachelor, with all the varieties of "freedom" that that state suggests. But now the shape of my world had changed. A whole set of transactions had occurred a year or two ago, carrying me along toward a Lady and with her toward the great sacrament that would offer to both of us the occasion to enact in ordinary daily life together the mightiest mysteries of all, namely, the mysteries that Williams called exchange, substitution, and coinherence. There had been private transactions (letters, conversations, trysts) and social transactions (visits to parents, parties, showers), then legal transactions (licenses, registers, blood tests), and finally ceremonial transactions (costumes, processions, solemn vows).

It was as though I had stepped into a picture and had met the Lady who had herself also stepped into this picture. It was myth brought home to us: myth, because it was the ancient story told everywhere and by everyone, always the same; brought home to us, because it was we who had stepped into it, all new and agog and unlettered, back then when we made our vows and went travelling and came back to find an apartment in this city.

We would not enact anything new. No married couple ever does. For us it would be the same round of ordinariness, the same rhythms of common life, that every other man and woman since Eden had enacted. Groceries, sheets and towels, silver and crystal and china, pots and pans, coats and hats, four walls and roof and door, stove and desk and bed: What else had anyone ever found around him? The coolie, the serf, and the Emperor of Byzantium had all had to cope with these same things one way or another. The chalice of chased gold and the clay mug were both variations of the single theme "cup". The tiled ovens full of dainty pasties and the smoking peat with the pot of gruel were both variations on the theme "food". The canopied and crested imperial couch and the dirty pallet of straw were both variations on the theme "bed". My lady and I could, of course, buy all these items at Woolworth's, the A&P, or

Bloomingdale's. We danced, nonetheless, with the Emperor and the serf—and with every clerk creeping from his flat in the Bronx and every cleaning woman leaving her tattered tenement full of fatherless children on 119th Street.

Who knew the steps to this dance? How was I doing?

Mighty poorly, no doubt.

Did the Jewish mother in the Bronx dance to the lead of her man, that clerk who crept out to his work every day? Did they know the choreography? And where was the father of those 119th Street children? How could that cleaning woman dance alone? Oh, somebody dance in here and show us the steps. Somebody fill in the missing places. Else we shall all stumble, and the dance will collapse. Anger and sorrow will come in where charity and joy should have been.

Was there anyone to dance in and fill up those gaps? Was there a dancer to assist the clumsy and prod the truculent and renew the exhausted?

There was an especially odd picture among the pictures on the Tarot cards. It was a picture of the Fool. His number was zero. You couldn't locate him with a number. He could go anywhere. Who was this Fool? Somebody, no doubt, who capered about, quite unpredictably, now here, now there, doing as he pleased and not accomplishing much of anything. After all, zero means worthlessness. No value at all is to be assigned to zero. Fools are like that.

Except that zero augments the numbers that have a value of their own. We use zero to designate tenfold, hundredfold, and thousandfold increases in value. And in ancient stories you often find a fool who is the only one about who talks sense. King Lear's fool was like that.

In his novel, Charles Williams fancied that the Fool sped twinkling through the Dance. All those odd pictures in the Tarot pack could, without entangling us in the occult at all, be taken to suggest figures in a dance—*the* Dance. The Hanged Man, Death, Justice, the Lovers—whatever they may mean to occultists, they are manifestly the big things that show up in ordinary experience, that is, in the Dance. But there is always something going wrong, something missing, something that foils our calculations. We can never get things quite right. Our best-laid schemes go awry. Sin and suffering and chance wreck our designs. People betray us, or we betray them, and it all turns into a muddle instead of a dance.

But the Dance holds together somehow. It holds together. No matter what shifts and shakings occur in the world, it goes on. Here, for example, are my Lady and I, beginning the very same dance that my grandfather began seventy years ago, and that his grandfather began seventy years before that; and yet the two worst wars in history have intervened to obliterate the world that my grandfather and his young bride knew. And yet my Lady and I begin the same steps. We are wed. The Dance goes on. And not just these solemn and joyous nuptial steps that she and I begin here, but all steps of all men. All the movements, joyous and sorrowful, of all men everywhere, and of sun and moon and stars, and of angels and archangels and all the company of heaven—they hold together. How?

Perhaps there is an unseen Dancer speeding here, there, everywhere, filling in the steps that are missed by us dancers. He would look ridiculous if you could waylay him for a moment—probably more like a fool than anything else. But perhaps there was something in those old rumors of the Fool. Perhaps that persistent idea of truth in the mouth of babes and sucklings (and fools) had something in it. There was foolishness about a crucifixion bruited abroad once upon a time, and it was thought to be so by the Greeks. Who knows what saving foolishness there might not be about? All that about somebody's bearing our griefs and carrying our sorrows.

Who was it? Who was it? Somebody is speeding through the Dance picking up burdens. Some Fool has undertaken to forgive our iniquities and heal our diseases. It is said that in him all things hold together. All DNA molecules? All orbits? All transactions and pacts? All grocery shopping and writing of dissertations and begetting of children? All.

The steps appointed to my Lady and me were the most common of all. They were to be found in the ordinary rhythms of domesticity: household tasks; out to work and back again; a man and a woman beginning, haltingly and awkwardly, to know each other; perhaps the nurturing of little children one of these days. Those were the steps.

These steps are held up to derision, even hatred, by powerful voices in our time, voices that want us to be liberated from it all as from bitter thralldom. But perhaps this thralldom is like the foolishness of the Fool. To a cursory glance, of course what he does looks like madness. Suffering for others forsooth! Taking guilt on yourself! By the same token, the steps in the Dance that he has appointed us (for is it not his Dance?) appear slavish to those who want their own dance. You have to obey in his Dance: that is patently slavish.

But there is an alchemy that transubstantiates the whole matter. It is the alchemy of the divine love. It turns all this leaden logic into the altogether riotous foolishness of pure gold. The Fool's self-emptying was, lo and behold, his exaltation. Obedience to the steps in the Dance is, lo and behold, liberty.

It is not, however, a secret doctrine for occultists or Tarot adepts. Ask the people who have loved. Ask those who have ever known the love of a kind and noble spouse. They will tell you what the liberators can't ever know, namely, that logic cannot any more come at the meaning of this than could Pontius Pilate's musings come at the meaning of the foolishness he was asked to decide about that day in Jerusalem.

10

The Infanta Comes

We had had two years or so of being able to close our door in the evenings and go out without having to organize babysitters. Presently it became apparent that we would have to reshuffle our categories.

Not for much longer would it be the independent little couple calling their own shots and designing their own existence in the big city. It was leap all the way into the human scene now, with diapers, plastic panties, feeding time, colic, cribs, potty chairs, prams, booties, and one thing and another.

In my bachelor days I would look at young couples in airports with their babies, and my soul would fill with horror. All this baggage. The babe in arms with sour milk dribbling down the front, leaning out in feverish, squalling dissatisfaction from his mother's arms, reaching petulantly into the air for he knew not what (and putting out a generally noxious miasma from both ends). And the two-year-old with a lollipop, wallowing on the floor, dragging at his mother's skirts. And the four-year-old with a dripping popsicle running down over his fist and chocolate smeared about his mouth, pulling his father to the newsstand to see some plastic Batman car. And the father all the while trying to riffle through the tickets to see what the flight number was, and the mother trying to keep tabs on the diaper bag, the stroller, the plastic car seat, the baby carrier, the folding bassinet, the bottle warmer, and the suitcases. Eheu! I thought. What does the human race think it is doing, procreating gaily away like this? Who are the clods who will opt for all this when you can be so patently free? After all, who's having the better holiday here, I with my one neat bag en route to Paris? or you all with all that crying mess heading for an awful vacation with your in-laws in a bungalow in Atlantic City?

Come at from that angle, it is difficult to find any rationale for the phenomenon. But you back into these things. It does not all gape upon you at once. First one thing happens (the child is conceived), then another (morning sickness, sleepiness), then another (maternity dresses), then another (natural childbirth classes), then another (the birthing). You don't suddenly find yourself one fine morning standing in LaGuardia beleaguered with a family. And the anxious bachelor has left one thing out of his reckoning: that beleaguered man loves that lady and those ragtag besiegers.

I cannot remember the early days after our discovery that we were no longer alone. I do remember that it had become more and more difficult for Lovelace to wake up in the morning. The question of pep medicine or iron pills may have flitted through our minds once or twice, but the doctor, somewhere along in there, said no. It's not anemia—it is what you think it is—and we hauled the sails around into the wind.

The immediate measures involved, for one thing, repeated trips on my part across Fourteenth Street (it started before we had moved) to Sixth Avenue to a carry-out Chinese food place. Chinese food seemed to be the thing craved. I would come back with eggrolls and waxed cardboard containers full of sweet-and-sour pork, sweet-and-sour chicken, rice, soup, and ersatz Szechwan goodies. (Later, with our second child, the great thing was to find chocolate cupcakes, cola, and hot dogs. We happened to be at a cottage in Aldeburgh on the North Sea when these cravings came on, and I set out on the sorrowful quest like Harry Belafonte looking all through the night for scarlet ribbons for his little daughter's hair, never for a moment supposing that such things could be found in Suffolk. But, like the scarlet ribbons he found just before the dawn was breaking, these unlikely items turned up in the shops, and I returned with joy bringing my sheaves with me. I felt like some great capering Saint Bernard dog wagging its tail and barking with pride as it leaps the last few steps, bringing the salvific keg of cognac to the frozen traveller.)

One of the things that happened in those early weeks of the new tack was that I set out one Sunday morning alone to scout out a church that we had heard about. We had visited a number of churches in the city, as churchgoing people are wont to do in a new place, and were still looking. We had seen in the *New York Times* on the page where all the churches announce themselves a little box giving the following information for one of the churches: "Catholic worship, liturgical music, gospel preaching". It was the Church of Saint Mary the Virgin, just off Times Square, known to its friends as Smokey Mary's. I had heard of this church before coming to the city and thought it might be an idea to visit it one day. I was not sure the incense would be the thing for Lovelace's present delicately poised gastronomic situation, so I set out alone.

I took the subway north to Times Square. This is a train that, on an early Sunday morning, looks very much like the Damnation Local. New York subways are bad enough at the best of times, but on a Sunday morning, when there are no passengers to validate the enterprise, there is nothing at all to

be said in their behalf. The train clanks and screeches balefully along, swaying and jolting violently over what must surely
be a raw rock roadbed. You sit in the wan dusk of the empty
car with newspapers and candy wrappers shifting about the
floor. A solitary derelict in a far corner slumps in a sodden
torpor. The sliding doors between the cars bang to and fro.
The train lurches to a halt at the stops, but no one gets on or
off. No traffic for hell today. Sometimes everything quiets
down completely, and you sit at one of these platforms with
the doors open, waiting. The compressed-air pump for the
brakes whirs on for a few seconds, but then that shuts off,
and there you are. Many times I have thought of walking
forward and accosting the motorman with "My dear fellow,
what, exactly, are we doing? Are you having coffee? Is there
a red signal? Are you testing the mettle of the passengers?
Are you under instructions to halt every twenty minutes this
way whether there is any reason to do so or no? I will pay
you an enormous sum of money if you will tell me." Somehow I never did this. The mien of New York subway mo-
tormen does not encourage this sort of sally.

If the subway is the Damnation Local, Times Square on a
Sunday morning lies somewhere in the precincts of perdition itself. One widespread picture of hell is of a region of
feverish activity, with great crowds of souls, worn out from
their bacchanalia, prodded on by demons, twittering about
in the ghastly search for one more diversion. You can see
this in the paintings of Hieronymous Bosch, or in Times
Square on any night. But surely the windy and vacuous des-
olation of Times Square on a Sunday morning, when it is all
over and no one but the odd straggler is left, is a far more
melancholy picture of perdition? On Saturday night at least
the illusion is still flying through the air like silver dust thrown
in our eyes. On Sunday morning the dust has settled into the

gutters, along with the spit and wet tissues, and what sparkled the night before gapes flatly at you in the blank light of day. Massage parlors, "adult" book shops, moth-eaten cinemas, pinball machine arcades, souvenir stands, and restaurants sit like stupefied whores, their makeup dulled and flaking after the night's work.

Saint Mary's stands half a block from Times Square. You can pass it easily enough without noticing it, since the facade is flush with the other buildings. If you do happen to look, you will see the gray stone and the nineteenth-century gothic of the doorways. If you go into the narthex and look down the nave aisle toward the high altar, you will see what most people expect to see in a church of ancient tradition: candles, crucifixes, arches, rich brocades, and all the furniture of the church.

You can find other furnishings—leatherette and formica and ashtrays—in the restaurants in Times Square, and there you can droop over the sticky counter nursing your coffee and trying to collect your wits. What a terrible hand of cards life has dealt me. How did I land here? Where is someone to lift this burden off me and love me?

There are no leatherette and formica here in Saint Mary's. Only this peculiar assemblage of ornaments and furniture, most of it spiky and uncomfortable, and all of it grossly out of date. You travel a thousand years when you step across this threshold. Everything in here has been assembled in obedience to a vision of things that seems remote indeed from the stark realities outside. It's real life outside there, surely: people creep into a church like this only as a last resort.

For me in that Sunday morning it was something like a visit to a shrine that one has heard about. The vestments, the music, the incense, the ceremonial—these were what people mentioned when they spoke of this church.

The Christian mysteries were celebrated that morning as they always are at Saint Mary's, and I, like all newcomers there, was overwhelmed. It was all very far removed from what you find in the "typical" American church, if by that we mean the white clapboard edifice that shows up in calendars of New England or on *Saturday Evening Post* covers. I was familiar with Christian rites that were plain, and this seemed lavish. The whole business of ceremony seemed to matter here. Every gesture seemed to carry some freight of significance. One minute the priest had his hands up like this, and the next they were out like that. One minute he was facing you, and the next he was sideways, and then he had his back to you. He even changed his vestments during the hour, from a cope to a chasuble. Nothing was natural or spontaneous or unstructured. In order to get from one place to another, they processed. They never merely *said* anything: it was all chanted. And nothing could be done without scattering smoke hither and thither. They walked around the altar with it, they swung it over books, shot it out at the priest, and finally waved it at us.

If everything else had put me off forever (which it hadn't), I would have gone back again for the music. All the antiphons were sung in Gregorian chant, the most pure, most austere of all musical forms, perfectly suited to the text of Scripture, since it liberates the words from the distracting style of any individual reader and sets them out, free from ornament, where there is nothing to do but listen to them. And the music of the Mass itself—the Kyrie, the Gloria, the Sanctus and Benedictus, and the Agnus Dei—was sung from a loft in the back of the church: no visible choir in robes, putting on a performance for us, but rather voices articulating these ancient canticles that utter the Church's response to the great mysteries of the gospel, and all of it sung, not by tremulous, warbling concert voices, but in that "white" tone, wholly free from vibrato, that again sets the text free from any individual's efforts to impress. And the hymns! Here were no racy, breathless tent-meetin' sentiments, dilating on one's private experience, nor any enfeebled twentieth-century World Council of Churches attempts at hymnody where you end up singing about nothing closer to the Christian mysteries than aspirations toward world brotherhood. No. Here were "Christ Is Made the Sure Foundation" and "Deck Thyself, My Soul, with Gladness" and "O Food of Men Wayfaring".

What is one to make of the liturgy? I thought. It is at a polar extreme from our era's attempts at getting things unstructured and spontaneous. A chance passerby might well think it is all horribly repressive and restricting. But what he would be missing would be the way in which all this structure, lo and behold, lifts us away from the poor little tiny circumference of our own private feelings and experience and liberates us into something that is infinitely more vast than ourselves—the way any great ceremony does. It is odd, how the whole race, in all tribes and cultures and centuries, has always resorted to ceremony—very carefully structured and elaborate ceremony—in the presence of life's deepest mysteries. Birth, marriage, and death: What do we all do with these purely organic, purely functional, events? We deck them and order them and set them about with ritual. Birthday cakes, wedding solemnities, funeral obsequies. What are they all about? Well, we are clearly ritual creatures. Perhaps our own era's efforts to replace pomp and ceremony with spontaneity are a tragic betrayal of the sort of creatures we are. The stars in their courses move in solemn dance; we read of seraphim and cherubim covering their faces in adoration; we see the whole world of flora and fauna repeating its yearly rituals in exuberant obedience to the rubric. Shall we, alone in the universe, insist that our freedom is to be found in the random, the ad hoc, and the unstructured? Surely one way of describing the difference between hell and the City of God is to say that the former is wholly unstructured and the latter magnificently structured?

I had, I thought, seen a diagram of that structured magnificence in the liturgy on that morning at Saint Mary's.

Pregnancy is intractable. Once it presents itself, there is no backpedalling. It comes on and settles down and spreads itself out all over things.

There came the night, finally, when the time was upon us. Lovelace was standing on a stool changing a lightbulb or cleaning a chandelier, when it became suddenly clear that everything else had to be set aside immediately.

There is a tempest of activity, with overnight bag, phone, elevator, taxi, and the trip across town, all tumbling over one another in your mind.

Roosevelt Hospital. It is a good hospital, you tell yourself. The best one in the city, they say. Ah—here we are at Ninth Avenue. Only a few more blocks to go now. Traffic is moving nicely this morning. Good. There's Lincoln Center there. The times we've had there. Usually we're getting out of the taxi there for the opera; this morning we stay in. Fordham University next. They're getting those new buildings up in a hurry. Saint Paul's Church. The Paulist Fathers. What an enormously high set of steps leading to the door. Here's Roosevelt.

I hope they've got their minds on what they're doing. I mean, here comes Mrs. Howard about to give birth. Are they ready? Suppose they've all been siphoned off by some emergency: maybe forty wounded firemen have just been brought in, and there's not a doctor free. Or maybe some freakish rush of mothers has arrived. After all, nobody is running the chance machine, spacing the arrivals out neatly so there are never more than two mothers needing the two delivery rooms at any given moment. What happens if ten mothers arrive together?

There goes a garbage truck round into Fifty-Eighth Street. Those guys couldn't care less about this. They've got a line of garbage pails along Fifty-Eighth Street there, and that's all they're interested in. Probably they're stopping for coffee. Here comes the street-sweeping machine. How do they ever get the gutters clean with all those cars parked illegally along here? The man just drives around them, obviously. He couldn't care less either—either about us and our baby or about the dirty gutters. He won't lie awake tonight because a pile of paper cups and dog mess got left under that Peugeot.

This whole city is just blithely going about its work as though nothing were happening. Those people crossing against the light, and those taxis zooming down Ninth Avenue, and these people hurrying along the sidewalk here. The day doesn't change for them just because *our* day has changed. Here we go, through these doors, and there goes a secretary out the doors to the Dunkin' Doughnuts place. One glazed, one cinnamon, and one plain. No sugar, just cream in my coffee. Napkins—don't forget napkins.

This way, past the reception desk there, along the linoleum to the elevators. That girl'll be sitting there at that desk with her ballpoint pen and nailfile the whole time we're up in the maternity ward. Twelve o'clock for her will mean that she can go to lunch. For us upstairs there it will mean that we are that much farther along in the process. Maybe eternity will have opened by then, and a child will have stepped through. Or maybe we'll be watching sweep hands, timing contractions. Or maybe something disastrous will have happened. There we'll be, tilting away at the interface between time and eternity with wrinkly, pale green gowns and masks for armor, and needles and wristwatches and pillows for arms.

What's on the far side of that interface? Do angels carry the child down? They never leave so much as a quill about if they do. But *this* business can't be the whole story—this muscle and tissue and blood, this pushing and straining and breathing. It's a birth. This child beginning her biography. A hundred years from now her great-great-grandchildren will be looking at scrapbooks: there's Papa's grandmother when she graduated from college. And there's his *great*-grandmother when she was one year old. They lived in New York. Her father taught school there. She became a famous novelist. They say she had a vocabulary of fourteen thousand words by the time she was seven. She picked it up from her father. He used to drop phrases like "remarkably maladroit" and "most earnestly to be deprecated", and she went around talking like that by the time she was seven.

But it's all occurring here in this place where they don't *know* us. The doctor does, in a way, of course: Lovelace has been seeing him now for eight months. He's very friendly. But then this is just Tuesday morning for him. Mrs.—um— Howard came in. But so did Mrs. Trogmeyer and Mrs. Throckmorton and Mrs. Thistlethwaite. They must know, though, that this is special. They must know that. They've all been waiting on tiptoe all these weeks. When's that baby coming? We'll run these others by in a hurry, but the one we've all been waiting for is this one. You can tell that this baby is going to be someone special.

It is hard to tell who is who around here, with everyone all muffled up in these unironed green sheets. You can't tell whether you are talking to a famous woman pediatrician or an orderly. They sail in and out with thermometers and pills and those gray blood-pressure straps. Here, take this.

No doubt all of them down the hall at the desk are talking about us. It's a big morning here at Roosevelt. Quite different from your average morning. Where's that nurse going with her coat on? *Off*? You mean she's just going to walk right out of here and go down the elevator and out into the street and on about her business as though all of New York weren't waiting motionless for this birth? What's she got to do that's so important? The hairdresser? Oh.

Things did not happen very quickly. I cannot remember now whether it was daytime or nighttime finally, but I remember a nurse giving me a pillow so that I could lay my head comfortably on the edge of the bed and sleep now and again. (Things get very quiet. The contractions recede. You both doze. You murmur every once in a while, You OK? M-hm. You? Mm. Any pains? None for a while now.)

Maybe nothing will happen. Maybe the whole thing will just go away. Why don't we do something else? This is a bore. Are we sure anyway that this is what we want? Maybe we're not ready.

But then inexorability looms, just as you drift off into this limbo. The pains pick up; the pressure increases; the cervix dilates; the top of the head presents itself, a little wet mat.

We'll go in now. Upsy-daisy. We'll just get you over onto this. There. All set. Yes, you can come too.

The thing that seems to be abroad in the delivery room is bonhomie. Teamwork. We're all here, and this is great. We know our job. We've done this lots of times before, and it's going to be fun. Is that comfortable now? Here—let me adjust this stirrup a little. That better? Good. Warm enough?

I tried to take up a position that would be knowledgeably unobtrusive (here, dummy: the *doctor* has to stand there) and at the same time would bespeak the tall, steady husband, right there with his wife, calm and strong through thick and thin. Next to her left shoulder seemed to get it about right. I kept my hand on her shoulder. That seemed to strike the right note. One couldn't help, really. They did all the pulling. It wasn't as though one could lend a hand in a tug of war.

Push now . . . harder . . . atta girl . . . great . . . it's coming . . . *c'mon* . . . ah!

The head. Face all squashed up. Odd color, aren't they. I mean, it is all right, isn't it? Shoulders. Arms, chest, stomach. Oh-oh—it's a girl, says the doctor. Are men supposed to want a boy first? The heir, the name, carry the family on, and so forth? Well, there's my daughter there. Daughter, late arrived from who knows where. Or how, for that matter. No storks have been seen flapping away with empty slings. No daubed coracles have been found washed up on the bank of the Hudson. No print of the messenger god's foot anywhere. None of that. Just linoleum and charts and the team of experts. But the deposit is the same. You get the same package whether it is the stork, Hermes, or Dr. Jones who brought it.

They handed her over to somebody who mopped her off. The rest has faded from my memory. Later we were in the corridor, and they had wrapped Lovelace neatly in a tan blanket like a mummy, with straps across the stretcher holding her in place. She looked dry and warm and safe.

Then pretty things began to happen. There are flowers and messages and visits, and everything all pink and white and ruffly. The mother has pretty bed jackets and the child pretty dresses. She had a tiny, petallike garment, too small to be called a dress, really. This was raiment for the child to come home in.

So there is the taxi again. Down the same elevator, past the girl at the desk (has she been waiting, excited, all week, to see what we have?) and out the glass doors. The taxi is a ceremonial car now; the mother is the Empress—get her in gently, attentively; the child is the Principessa, all arrayed in minuscule and fragrant splendor there; let the grandmother and grandfather sit, one on the right hand and one on the left, in places of honor. The father will just pop into the front here by the meter, agile, eager, self-effacing. This hippie at the wheel will have to serve for coachman.

Now we move out into the avenue. *Ware! Ware!* The Infanta comes! The Dauphine! The Heiress-presumptive! Fall back, men of the city! Press back there! Peek from your shutters, oh, ye beldames and duennas! Fly into alleys, ye urchins and ragamuffins! Hear the bells peal loud and joyous and the trumpets sound high and sweet. Stand tall, ye corsairs, cossacks, and ghurkas. Prance and nod your plumes, ye matched grays. Nay, let all the earth rejoice!

The dents in the fenders, the cigarette ashes on the seats, the folded newspaper and cigar box of change, the dashing ahead and jockeying for position at red lights, and the creeping along behind that United Parcel truck: these are mirages. We come, we come! And here are the doormen, springing to welcome and assist the newborn beatitude.

The Inexorable Summons

The rhythms in the household change now. They slow down and deepen, the way a brook does when it comes into a pool after twinkling helter-skelter over the pebbly shallows. You find that a center of gravity is making its claim.

For one thing, there are more people now. Three is a crowd. It is a throng. For it is not as though the complexity of life has been increased by a simple fifty percent. It has shot up logarithmically, and suddenly the smallest items tower and loom.

Eating and drinking, for example, or falling asleep: these are activities that the adult world fits into its other concerns quite neatly. But with the newborn there is no fitting these activities into anything else at all. These *are* the concerns.

Take eating and drinking. They are combined for the first few months, but do not imagine that you have saved time and trouble thereby. There is an inverse ratio at work whereby the combined activity turns out to be far, far more demanding than the two separate ones. One would think that with everything arranged so conveniently nothing could be simpler. Here, child: Are you hungry? Everything is all set. Go to it. And the whole process over in a trice.

But no. For one thing there is the imperious frequency of the business. The child has eaten (or drunk, whichever you will) and is back in her crib, and Mama in her kerchief and Papa in his cap have just settled down for another furtive nap snatched from the jaws of nursery life when the hue and cry is raised again. Or so it seems. Actually, four hours *have* passed. But they seem a niggardly span when you find them between 1:00 and 5:00 A.M.

And again, there is not only the frequency but also the unsatisfactory nature of the business. The child won't *do* it right. First there are fretting and fooling about with the breast, and then she won't stick at it. Her attention wanders. And it is not as though you can dandle trinkets or stuffed monkeys in front of her to attract her: the whole point is to coax her attention back to the matter at hand, not lure it away. When she does dawdle back to the fount, it turns out that she is not getting anything. She does not seem to have picked up the knack. Or, when she does get something, you find a stream of curds suddenly pouring down the front. She has spit it all up. Mop that up, coax more into her, and she drifts off to sleep. You tiptoe gingerly back to the crib with her and put her back down, praying that she has gotten enough to last another four hours, and tiptoe back to bed. Dear Lord, please help me to be able to sleep for just half an hour here before I must get up for breakfast and leave for work—ai-ai-ai-ai! Oh. Whatever can be the trouble now?

Colic. Pains. Some infants are sunny and phlegmatic and do not get colic. Both of ours, stemming as they did from a double lineage of agitated, fierce, and volatile people, hadn't a chance. Their guts were pinched, plucked, and bedevilled with dyspepsia from the start. There was no question of food being digested with any equanimity. It was all guns blazing and all flags flying all the way.

My mother had had a method for getting babies with colic to simmer down. You lay them face down across your knees, over a barrel, as it were. Then you jog your knees, briskly or gently as indicated, back and forth, all the while thumping them on the back. Their legs churn, and their arms wave, and they try to pick up their heads and look about. Presently they burp. It is one of the sweetest sounds in the world. I had become quite good at the technique, having practiced it on innumerable nieces and nephews.

But feeding the child is far from being the end of your work. The corollary to eating and drinking is digestion. There is always some detritus, no matter how good a child's digestion is, and this must go. It is one of the implacable data like birth itself: something has to happen sooner or later. You cannot simply decide to forego the business.

Now the child, truculent though she may be about getting food in, is blithe enough about getting it out and does so with zest at all times and in all places through every available orifice. Here there are diapers—lovely piles of them, all snowy and folded and stacked. But there are, by the same token, buckets of them, all befouled and sodden and fermenting. The miasma that floats from a diaper bucket cannot be disguised no matter what fumigants, antitoxins, and essences are invented. You can tell the moment you walk into a house whether an infant lives there. The unmistakable scent hangs in the air. They have made things as neutral and immaculate as possible for us now by inventing paper throwaway diapers, and it must be confessed that flushing things all the way down drains rather than sousing them up and down is an enormous advantage.

But you are never very far from having to change a diaper when there are infants about. I became fairly adept at it— again, I had had practice on my nieces and nephews. There is a certain satisfaction in pinning a baby, all cleansed and powdered, back together again, but you know that this, like life's other satisfactions, is ephemeral. You will be at it again presently.

And then there is the business of getting to sleep. Lovelace, being the mother, had the mother's natural alarm clock that trips off with the slightest irregularity of breathing on the part of the infant. I was only the father, but coming as I did from that volatile lineage, I tended to be on the *qui vive* all the time anyway and hence shared her vigilance. Sleep was a fugitive affair at the best of times, and now with an infant in the house we lay down with all antennae aquiver and were halfway through the apartment like a shot at the smallest snuffle from the child's room. But the matter of the parents' sleep is not the major difficulty. The great thing is to get the child to sleep on any sort of schedule.

We have many friends whose infants are bland, amiable creatures who appear to have arrived without taint of original sin. They coo and burble contentedly, then fall into the most pastoral of torpors, not to move or awaken for twelve hours. Ours, in contrast, are hag-ridden by every terror and anxiety ever laid on the race of Adam. Hence there was not much question of anyone's drifting off to sleep on any rose-petal skiff. You feed them, then, if the pangs of colic have not struck, you lay them over your shoulder and begin patting, rocking, and singing softly. You sing the most soporific lays you can think of, and you slowly decelerate the pace, hoping fervently that some sort of hypnotism will thereby take effect. Finally, in a transport of suspense, you stop for a moment. Ah. The child sleeps.

Hey, nonny! Up pops the head, and loud sounds the pibroch. We are wide awake, and not only awake but nettled as well. Pray, what do you mean by leaving off your lullaby like that? This is a fine showing!

But it is not all diapers and curds and colic. This summons to the center is a lure as well. It is as though something quarried from that center has appeared suddenly and has been placed in your trust. A precious pearl withouten spot.

There are things that the couple in the airline terminal cannot tell the bachelor off on his lark with his little valise. Would they, for ten thousand kingdoms, change their luggage for his? Would they be set free from their shackles there? Here—shall we snatch these tiresome creatures from your skirts and send them off to the salt mines? You'll be free then. Shall we slaughter the innocents at a stroke? There's emancipation for you. There's lib, quick and total.

No. No, no, no. Give us back our children, and all the diaper pails and vigils into the bargain. The burden is light—or at least it's heavy, but we are freer with it on our backs and clinging to our breasts than we ever dreamed we could be before it was laid on us.

There are things hard to be told because they defy all calculating. They fly in the face of all that is reasonable. How can it possibly be urged that to sit at home night after night like this is to be preferred to stepping out here, there, and the other place? Wouldn't you *rather* be out on the boulevard than sitting in here? Think of all the beautiful people and all the magnificent events you are missing. Did you see Nureyev and Fonteyn at the opening night last Tuesday? And have you seen the new Robbe-Grillet film? My *dear*! And you must pop down to The Electric Circus one night; it's too divine. And by the way, absolutely everyone who is anyone is showing up at La Côte Basque now. You can't not appear. And you must see the rooms they've got now on the sixth floor at Bloomingdale's. You'll go mad. Oh—we're having a little do at Easthampton next weekend. Can you make it?

Thanks. Thanks awfully. It's very kind. You see, we . . .

But how do you speak to the boulevard about these things? How do you tell the brook babbling over the pebbles that the quiet pools are also part of the watercourse? How shall the Sister of Saint Vincent de Paul win the attention of

Madison Avenue? What window display will she set up to galvanize the passersby? A rosary and a bedpan? How shall the teacher of deaf children bid against Elizabeth Taylor or Jacqueline Onassis for lifestyle excitement quotients? How shall the priest tell us why he is getting up in the cold dawn to stand before the altar saying fixed formulas that are repeated thousands of times every day all over the world anyway? Good heavens! Life is so short! Don't let yourself get becalmed in one of these backwaters with the rush and twinkle of the rapids just racing past you.

But odd things happen in backwaters. Bethlehem, for example, was a backwater.

We bought an enormous dark blue high-wheeled pram, and Lovelace would go out shopping pushing this great phaeton in front of her with the baby arranged among the pillows and blankets, and the terrier in the little carrier bag attached to the rear of the vehicle. This little entourage would come up the street to meet me at the end of my day at school, and we would walk home through Central Park, parallel to the street. White-uniformed nannies are there pushing majestic prams along, and painted old women coaxing disgruntled pugs along on leashes. Flotillas of racing bikes sweep past with the riders bent double over the handlebars. Joggers in gray sweatsuits puff past. A mounted policeman clops along. The sycamore leaves are blowing off now and scud around under your feet. Here is one of the lovely faces of New York, and you feel for a moment as though the little rhythm of your domestic scene can touch and mesh with the big rhythm of the city. You are part of the whole pageant. Here comes the prep school teacher, home from a day in the classroom, walking along with his wife, his child, and his dog. They're part of this tableau here in Central Park.

Often on Saturdays we would go abroad into the Park to join the throngs in their weekend leisure. The mayor had had the park closed to all motor traffic on weekends, so it was a great promenade on Saturdays and Sundays. We would enter just above the Metropolitan Museum and walk south about fifteen blocks to Seventy-Second Street. You pass the Hans Christian Andersen statue, and the Alice in Wonderland statue, and the little pond where boys sail their toy sailboats. Then you come to the great balustrade overlooking the fountain and the boating lake. It is very Parisian here, with gay awnings and little tables where you can sit and nibble guacamole and sip sangria. A brisk air of camaraderie presides over everything.

Once when I was cycling alone through the park, I was whistling one of Papageno's arias from *The Magic Flute*. I whistled up the scale of a certain measure and paused, whereupon another cyclist filled in the remaining phrase. Bravo! I thought. Here is what we all want in this big city: Harmony. Camaraderie. Peace and happiness.

And indeed there are moments here and there when you are able to forget, briefly, the surliness and snobbery and slovenliness that seem generally to mark existence in that city and to suppose that, given a chance, everyone would turn out to be as amiable and innocent as the optimists have always told us we are. It is no doubt this hope that lies at the root of the efforts to free people from their isolation by means of T-groups and happenings and intimacy jamborees such as you find at Big Sur or in Central Park on a hot day, when people suddenly decide to take off their clothes. Back to our natural innocence and our ability to relate freely to each other.

And it is no doubt from this viewpoint that the exactness and rigor of, say, family loyalties look villainous. Is not this the problem? Is not the thing that is making us all bristle and snarl at each other just this fortress attitude that the human race has taken up, with every one of us having built earthworks around our little castle, prepared to defend our small circle against all comers? Surely it is just another case in point of the private property error.

So goes the argument. And it is mightily plausible, no doubt, if what we want is a perpetual jamboree or happening or orgy. But if it is right, then of course every tribe and civilization since Eden has had it all wrong, since they have all been built on the assumption that any conceivable ordering of things begins by granting the family unit and moves out from there. Even the hearty experiments in gigantic communal living in places like Russia and China have ended up having to make concessions, not to say capitulate, to this strange and persistent human inclination to come home to spouse and children.

By the time we left New York, it was becoming common to hear loudly proclaimed in angry articles and angry speeches that domestic fidelity and that sort of thing were bourgeois and that a great deal of the sickness we find in our society may be laid at the feet of traditions and conventions like that.

But the householder would want to ask, ever so hesitantly, whether we are quite sure that this *is* what is wrong with everything. Is it the man's love for this one woman that has taught him to be selfish and predatory? Is it her love for him that has dried up the springs of charity in her? Indeed, where you find love like this, do you find predatoriness and uncharity? Has their love for their children made them pusillanimous? Is their children's experience of this love in turn teaching them to be ignoble? Is it the parents' fidelity to these bonds that has made them surly and suspicious of everyone else? Is this really what we find when we look through the annals of family life?

Might there be some paradoxes in there by which the people who had "shut themselves in", as it were, inside the walls of fidelity and trust were, oddly, the people who had begun to learn about charity? Were these the ones who had learned, in the schooling of domestic faithfulness, something about what is really at stake in approaching and knowing all other selves? Did the spouse faithful to his nuptial vows know more, perhaps, about openness to others than the barfly? Did the virgin faithful to her vows to her community know good things that the woman who has been liberated into random relationships didn't know? Will it be the monk, chaste for the sake of his intercessory ministry in behalf of the whole human family, or the lecher, plowing every field in sight, to whom I will turn in my trouble?

So, presently, for us there were fewer dazzling variations on the theme of daily life. There were fewer pyrotechnics. One might say there were fewer fortissimo and vivace passages. You are in the andante movement now, and, as with the late quartets of Beethoven, sequence and harmony are all. There is less to catch the fancy of the dilettante.

I think it was while we lived in New York that the phrase "lifestyle" somehow came into English vocabulary, presumably from the sociological quarter. Our lifestyle was indistinguishable from that of thousands upon thousands of other New Yorkers, and of city dwellers all over the world. We belonged, I suspect, to the silent majority in the sense that we did not show up in any of the categories that engage public interest. We were not jet set or society, so we did not show up in Suzy Knickerbocker's columns. We were not radical chic, so we did not get lampooned by Tom Wolfe. We were not political activists, so the television cameras never peered our way. We were not minority (actually we were: WASPs are the smallest of all minorities in New York), so political candidates, pundits, and sociologists were not excited by us. We were not trendsetters, so the glossy magazines never rang us for interviews.

Our lifestyle was, I say, indistinguishable from that of thousands of people all over the Bronx, Brooklyn, Staten Island, Queens, and Manhattan. Up; breakfast; out to work for the father; stay home and shop, mop, and tend the baby for the mother; home for supper; putter about in the evening; bed. And meanwhile the child growing from bassinet to crib, from lap to highchair, from nipple to spoon, from lace to corduroy.

We had another child, a son, while we lived there. He arrived, after an ambiguous pregnancy, eleven weeks early, weighing two pounds, thirteen ounces. He had, into the bargain, a polysyllabic blood problem, so they put his incubator under bright fluorescent lights for a day or two (that is the cure). This involved their bandaging his eyes so that when we would go into the room to see him all in our gowns and masks, there he would be, a tiny, naked waif, looking for all the world like a plucked chicken dressed up as a Civil War veteran.

The chances of his surviving the night of his birth were dim, of course, so I rang up our priest at midnight (we had in the meantime become parishioners at Saint Mary's) and asked him if he could come along and baptize the child. He arrived, and he and I put on hospital gowns, scrubbed, and were admitted to the sanctum where they kept the incubators. You have to give a name to a child being baptized, so, not wanting to bury all the nice family names we had had picked out for a presumptive son, I pulled one out of the air. The priest took a little paper cup from a dispenser there, and, putting his hands through the portholes in the plexiglas of the incubator, baptized the child according to the formula used by all of Christendom from the beginning.

What did this have to do with anything? Would it have made any difference if we had not done it? A bit of water from a paper cup poured onto the scalp—how do you connect that with the plastic tubes taped to the child's face and running through his nose to his stomach? Will these tepid drops help him somehow? Shall we enter it on his chart as one of the measures taken to assist in getting his life launched? (Perhaps there ought to be a box somewhere on the chart, along with Temperature and Blood Pressure and Pulse, for Mumbo-Jumbo, where soothsayers and fairy godmothers and priests may check what *they've* done, just to keep the record complete.)

No, says the mind of Christendom. It is not medical science at work here, but it is not magic either. It is sacrament. It is an act that stands on the cusp between the things you can see and the things you can't and that affirms the unity of the whole design. It is not science, since it opens out onto mysteries that elude the calculations of science; but it is not magic either, since there is no attempt to manipulate things here the way you do with magic. Nothing is being conjured here. The molecules of the water do not carry a tiny freight of grace with them that percolates through the scalp into the brain and thence to the soul somehow. The water is necessary first of all because the dominical command enjoins it. But the command was not a caprice, calling for merely random ingredients. Water, from the beginning, seems somehow to have been the agent, or at least the sign, even the medium, by which the redemption proclaimed in the Christian gospel is brought home to us. From the prehistoric moving of the Holy Spirit upon the chaotic waters, through the Flood, the Red Sea, Jordan, and the baptism submitted to by Christ and preached by the apostles, water has been there, the sacrament of salvation somehow. Who knows how? Like all sacraments, it faces both ways: toward us, bringing the mystery home to us; and toward the mystery where we cannot penetrate. Why it should be water and not milk, or honey, or even wine has not been explained to us. But somehow, the ordinary, perishable stuff water participates in the process.

Christendom will always have to say "somehow", since it is neither science nor magic that is at work in sacrament, and those are the two poles to which our imaginations tend to fly when we are up against the inexplicable. The sacraments are neither of these. They do not suddenly bring about startling effects. No one is transported by them from one place to another, or even from bad habits to good habits. There is nothing automatic about them. No one has ever been able to work out any wholly satisfactory formula as to how they work.

We, unable in a moment in a hospital corridor to sort out what the doctors of the Church have been at for centuries, did what Christians do. We bowed to the teaching and example of the Church. Not disposed to come at these mysteries as though no one had ever thought of the difficulties before, we took our signals from the tradition of the Church. It was not as though we could flip open a Bible and find an answer that had somehow escaped everyone else. Whatever the opinions on the question, we could at least say that most of the Church for most of her history has understood and practiced it thus. Latin Fathers, Greek Fathers, and Reformers—these at least had taught Christians to bring their newborn to the font. In this case the font had to come to the newborn. But the child was baptized. We were in the presence of a great mystery there at the incubator.

We now had two summonses to the center, as it were. Our eldest summons was almost three, so that meant she had to walk, or ride on my back in a canvas-and-aluminum frame, when we went out for walks. The pram now carried the infant son. And there were four of us at the table now, or rather three, with the fourth in the highchair presently. There were now two bedrooms from which cries for help might come at night. Two sets of clothes to shop for in children's departments, and two sets of toys and books to buy for Christmas. There were two claimants to lap space, and two sets of lullabies to sing.

What were we being hailed with here, with all this pink softness and dependence? What were these tiny creatures who were so breakable and who depended so unabashedly on us? The scene that I left in the mornings as I set out for work was of sunlight streaming through the thin, stretched, white curtains down onto the rug, with the dog settled onto the yellow corduroy sofa next to the little girl with her picture books and the infant in his highchair with his spoon and cream of wheat. Over it all presided the mother, moving about doing the little morning things. Couldn't one just curl up here and let the world hang itself in its own toils? The bankers and lawyers being picked up in limousines down below on Park Avenue, and the truck drivers banging their tailgates over on the West Side, and the classrooms full of frenetic boys—those *things* would all have to take care of themselves. Let me just close my door and find my world here in this spot of morning sunlight. It is hard to be boosted out into the maelstrom and tumult.

But the summons to the center did not, surely, mean an invitation back to the womb. Perhaps these antiphonal demands—of attendance on the one shrine and of going out to provide for the ones who lived there—asked an obedience to a rhythm that would turn out to be the rhythm of the very Dance for which we were made. Perhaps these ancient, common rhythms to which all men and women had danced from the beginning would turn out to be the bearers of power and love and joy.

How else was one to discover what he was made for? How, for example, shall a trumpet know what his silver coils are about until fanfares and tuckets are blown through him? How shall a cello learn what his gut strings and cavernous hollowness are for until he is forced into the rigors of the Beethoven string quartet? How shall a petrel know what his wings are for until he is nudged out of the nest onto the bosom of the tempest?

Men had been going off to work after breakfast for thousands of years. All men everywhere had been going off to work like this. The Chinese silk merchant, the Tenth Avenue truck driver, the Hottentot, the banker, the teacher, nay, the Cro-Magnon hunter himself: they all had to get up and go out through the door (or the flap, or the beaded curtain, or the mouth of the cave). What burdens they carried! What tracking of foes, what trapping of prey, what blazing of trails, what sailing over horizons, what felling of trees, what coping with traffic, what toiling through committees, what writing of books. What sharpening of blades, what quarrying of boulders, what raising of towers, what gnawing at pencil ends, what shuffling through papers. And all for what?

Well, to get bread and milk onto the table, for one thing. Whatever visions and ambitions pricked them on otherwise, they had at least to do this. At their backs as they went out to meet the Huns or the students stood their wives and children. Happy creatures at home! Ah, the hearth! Ah, haven, sheltered from all the burly-burly and strife. Ah, the peace and freedom the goodwife must know, defended as she is by this princely husband of hers. Ah, the nonsense that goes through that husband's imagination.

It is as nonsensical as the trumpet supposing that the coils alone were responsible for the fanfare, without the mouthpiece. It is as though the strings on the cello congratulated themselves that the quartet was sounding from them alone, without the sounding board. It is as though the petrel's right wing credited himself alone with the bird's glorious flight, ignoring the left wing.

Who, for example, had carried for nine months entirely alone a burden that her husband could not share at all? Who had suckled these creatures, day and night, without ever being spelled off? Who presided over the whole perpetual motion of the household? Who sat at the very center point of the whole turning? Who knew in her very marrow the mysteries that her spouse strove at a distance to descry?

This is a picture of things that is under assault now. The main objection is that this ordering of things is not fair. And no doubt it *is* unfair—to both parties. That a man should be trammeled this way and obliged to spend his hard-won money on these people, and to return to the same table and bed every night, and to have his important time taken up with the concerns of women and children; or that a woman should be in thrall to all these domestic trivialities when she has all these other capacities to offer to the world: it is patently unfair. Clearly the entire human race has had it wholly wrong from the start. Oh, the millennia of injustice to be made up for!

So goes the assault. The response—now let us see . . . what *is* the response? The criticism is so manifestly true, so utterly plausible. There can be no response except to agree. Come here a moment, Dear: this person wants to set us free from our prison. Shall we go? The thing is, I'm not sure that our liberator hasn't got into the wrong place. I mean, it's a prison that he supposes he has dashed into, and prisoners he thinks he is addressing. He is really quite convinced. How shall we show him his mistake? Perhaps if we could get him to sit down at our table . . .

O Ordinariness, Where Is Thine Ordinariness

On Sunday mornings we always went out to church in a taxi. It was a routine for us as it is for hundreds of millions of people and has been for two millennia now.

It is easier perhaps to keep small children interested at a church such as ours was than it is in churches where there is no liturgy, since in ours there was always something going on. Here there was a procession of crucifer, acolytes, thurifer, deacon, subdeacon, celebrant, and ceremoniarius. Then water was sprinkled everywhere at the asperges; then smoke billowed up from the thurible as the grains of incense were cast onto the coals; and all of it was done by men in gorgeous raiment, with the choir chanting the antiphons, then singing the music of the Mass. And all of us, all the while, up and down, first standing, then kneeling, then sitting.

Why bother to take children? We took our daughter to be baptized at the Mass not long after her birth, and from then on she came with us. Shortly before we moved away from the city our son, just out of the incubator, came for his first time, to be presented at the Mass, having already been baptized on the night of his sudden birth. But children cannot begin to grasp the great mysteries that are enacted in the Christian liturgy. Is it not a travesty to bring them to a spectacle like this?

No, says the mind of Christendom. If we take children to a Fourth of July parade long before they are able to grasp the issues that divided George III from the Continental Congress, or show them the crêche long before they have come to terms with the mystery of the Incarnation, we may likewise bring them here where there is enacted day by day the whole story of the gospel that we want them to know and love above all else in the world.

What is it that we wanted our two to know as a result of our having taken them to church? Or, put another way, what would we want to hear them say they knew if, some day when they are adults, we were to ask them what they now understood by the liturgy that they had known since infancy?

We would want them to know that here they were assisting at the act that is at the very center of all Christian vision—the act that, in obedience to the dominical command, the Church has celebrated without ceasing, day in and day out, century after century, through all the tumult of history.

And we would want them to know that it was an *act*, not merely an experience. They did not come here to receive a beautiful worship experience. They came to do something. What they came to do was to worship and adore. If there can have been planted deep in their young imaginations the sight of men and women and children offering obeisance to the Most High, then something will have been achieved, since they will grow up in a world to which the idea of such obeisance is demeaning. They will be told that liberated men and women do not bow down before anything. But if they have seen and know what public, deliberate acts of worship look like, they will at least have something lodged in their imagination that might qualify what they are hearing from their world.

And we would want them to know that solemnity, or ceremony, or ritual, far from being a Procrustean bed into which we force our natural spontaneity, thus killing any life, is, on the contrary, the very ordering and structuring that our humanness cries out for. Just as language, so often tossed about in slang and idle chat, cries out for the liberty and perfection to which it is brought by poetry; or as a body, so often allowed to slump into fat, cries out for the spring and mastery to which it is brought by gymnastics; or a brain, so often wasted in daydreaming and triviality, cries out for the power and brightness to which it is brought by the discipline of logic and rhetoric; so our capacity to worship and adore, so often dissipated by the fluctuations of our feelings of the moment, cries out for the solidity and articulateness to which it is brought by the liberating office of the ritual. It is a paradox, of course, that an exacting form (the liturgy) imposed on something spontaneous (our wish to worship) should set it free rather than imprison it. But the same paradox is visible all through human experience: the child is set free not by being permitted to do whatever he pleases but by discipline; the lover is set free not by being given a license for lechery but by the nuptial bond.

And we would want them to know that everything that occurs in the liturgy is an enactment of what is true. It is not a program or a multimedia presentation. It is an enactment, exact and austere, of all the mysteries of the gospel. We would want them to know from the start that enactment itself is deeply in the human grain: all brides coming down aisles, all bowing of heads to say grace, all hands raised to wave hello or goodbye—these are all enactments; for even in small gestures we acknowledge the principle that it is appropriate, even significant, to signal something that is true by a physical act. There are other, more convenient ways, for a bride to get to where the groom is standing, but we feel that it is significant to do it this way since there is a great deal at stake. Grace can be said at the table with everyone holding their heads high, but we feel that the gesture of bowed head, which is really a movement of our neck muscles, bespeaks the idea of subjects in the presence of their Lord and that this is worth doing. It is a principle that we acknowledge with almost every breath and that is at work in this most significant of all enactments.

We would want them to know that in these solemnities they are invited to participate in the highest of mysteries, namely, the Sacrament in which Christ, by his own promise, gives to his people his Body and Blood. For here everything is brought to a point. The Sacrifice in which he offered himself *for* us is made present in this Bread and Wine in which he offers himself *to* us; and, in the mystery of exchange, he receives the bread and wine that we bring to his altar together with ourselves and gives them back to us as Food from his table. Whether it is a High Mass like this or the Mass of a missionary priest in a hut, it is the same thing. All is gift. All is largesse. We bring our sins, and they are taken away by his oblation of himself. We bring our selves, all unworthy, and they are taken and received as living sacrifices by the virtue of his one Sacrifice of himself once offered. We bring our bread and wine, and they are made his Body and Blood for us for our salvation.

And we would want them to see that in this act there is gathered up and focused all the activity of the week. That which is celebrated here, namely, Substitution and Exchange—his life laid down in our behalf—is the principle that is to be at work in all the humdrum routines of our life and work during the rest of the week. For unless that principle animates what we do, we will find it all quickly fragmenting into cupidity, frustration, and inanity. The commonplaces of our daily life may become modes of either heaven or hell to us. Felicity or anger. Health or debility. It depends on whether we are clutching at them to see what we can wring for ourselves from them or offering them up to be taken into the only Oblation there is and transformed. As often as we assist at the liturgy, we are helped on our way in this ordering of things by being ourselves taken into the sacramental presence of that one Oblation by which the world is redeemed from cupidity, frustration, and inanity.

It is as though we are here vouchsafed a vision, clear and bright, of that Center to which we are summoned, summoned, summoned, day in and day out, by all the occasions and duties we find laid upon us. Here there is opened up and displayed that which is hinted and guessed at in every commonplace exchange of the week. At the Center there are Substitution and Exchange. At the Center there is self-offering. At the Center there is gift. Here ordinary things are changed. That which is given away is received back changed: duty is transformed into largesse, obedience becomes liberty, and death itself is swallowed up in victory. O death, where is thy sting? O ordinariness, where is thine ordinariness?

But if this is so, then blessed, praised, celebrated, magnified, exalted, glorified, and hallowed be the Name, and the commemoration, the memory, and every memorial of it both now and forever, as the ancient bidding has it. How shall we compass mysteries like this? How shall we hail splendors like this? What alleluias will utter the praise, what smoke will bespeak the holiness, what bowings will acknowledge the majesty, what processions will proclaim the triumphs, what hymns will declare the honor, due the Name of the One who was slain and is alive forevermore?

Here comes an empty cab now, I think. Good. In you get. We can all squeeze into the back—here, I'll hold Charles while you get in; then Gallaudet can sit on my lap. Have you got the diaper bag? Look out—she's getting crumbs all over. Eighty-Seventh and Park, driver. Probably straight across to Madison and up is the best. Yes, I've got loads of room. What about you, my Lady?